Annabel's
Family Cookbook

Annabel's
Family Cookbook

100 simple, delicious recipes that everyone will enjoy

ANNABEL KARMEL

EBURY
PRESS

For my children Nicholas, Lara and Scarlett
and my dogs Hamilton, Bono and Sabre,
without whom no family would be complete.

10 9 8 7 6 5 4 3

Published in 2014 by Ebury Press,
an imprint of Ebury Publishing.

A Random House Group Company.

The Random House Group Limited Reg. No. 954009

Addresses for companies within the Random House
Group can be found at www.randomhouse.co.uk

A CIP catalogue record for this book is available from
the British Library

Penguin Random House is committed to a sustainable
future for our business, our readers and our planet.
This book is made from Forest Stewardship Council®
certified paper.

To buy books by your favourite authors and register
for offers visit www.randomhouse.co.uk

Design: Smith & Gilmour
Photography: Martin Poole
Food stylists: Annie Rigg and Laura Fyfe
Stylist: Lydia Brun

Colour origination by Altaimage, London
Printed and bound in China by C&C Offset
Printing Co., Ltd

ISBN: 9780091957667

CONTENTS

Introduction

I LOVE FOOD. I adore being in the kitchen; but most of all, I relish family mealtimes. My most precious memories of my three children growing up revolve around the dinner table; chit-chatting about our day, our friends, our three dogs, our funny stories – anything to get us talking and sharing.

It was an incredibly positive way of teaching them about the art of conversation and, in equal measure, about listening. Freedom of speech was always encouraged, and I believe those democratic mealtimes helped us to become a close family. But cooking regular healthy meals while setting up and growing my food business wasn't easy by any stretch of the imagination. Amongst juggling after-school activities, homework, returning calls and catching up with my ever growing to-do list, I had to prep dinner and serve up a meal for three fussy children, which everyone would eat and enjoy. It's no wonder that sitting down to a home-cooked meal is a rarity for so many families.

The truth is, family mealtimes are an important part of happy, healthy living. Time and time again studies show that when families come together at the dining table, they tend to eat more of the good stuff – fresh vegetables, fruit and nutrient-rich ingredients. Rushing around, 'making do' and grabbing food on the go can all lead towards unhealthy eating habits such as snacking, skipping meals, eating fast food and fussy eating.

Establishing a kitchen table routine from an early age will help encourage a healthy diet for life. Varied, well-balanced meals provide your growing family with all the minerals and vitamins they need to develop.

My children are now in their early twenties but they are still the first to claim a place at the dinner table. The girls still live at home, which I put down to always having a supply of yummy food in the house; delicious smells emanating from the kitchen is part of what makes any house a welcoming home. What's more, all those mealtimes spent conversing over my family-sized fish pies and stir fries have blessed them with a love of good, wholesome food. They unplug themselves from the lure of modern digital life to talk, laugh and put the world to rights.

We cannot underestimate the power of eating good food together; but where to start when life is so hectic? A lack of inspiration coupled with choc-a-block schedules could mean your family is missing out on lots of exciting new tastes and flavours, let alone a whole range of nutrients.

That's where my *Family Cookbook* comes to the rescue. You don't have to be a Cordon Bleu chef. You won't need special skills, expensive equipment or obscure ingredients. Very simply, it's a beautifully illustrated collection of my favourite easy-to-follow family recipes.

Fast dishes such as my super tasty Sesame Beef Stir Fry (page 44) and Potato & Chicken Rösti (page 33) are ideal for when hungry mouths just won't wait. When time is tight, food needs to fit around you – and these ultra-quick, nourishing recipes using everyday kitchen cupboard ingredients are easy wins, and will ward off any temptation to forage for naughty snacks.

The secret to stress-free cooking is finding foods that everyone will enjoy. My own recent research indicated that one in four mums are producing up to 63 meals a week to suit their family's palettes – it would seem that household kitchens are becoming more like cafes! It's so important to find meals that suit the whole family plus have that essential magical ingredient: 'child appeal'.

While feeding the children separately may seem like an easy solution to keep the kids content, all that extra time spent in the kitchen rustling up a menu of meals could be spent eating together at the table – and my book offers simple food solutions that everyone will want to eat. Sticking to a set mealtime can be tricky, but I always tried to organise three or four regular mealtimes during the week where we all sat down together.

Children like to copy grown-ups, so eating with them is the perfect opportunity to try new foods, practice good table manners and develop their social skills. For Monday to Friday food inspiration, flick to my Everyday Meals chapter which is brimming with easy recipes that deliver maximum satisfaction with minimum preparation. My Tasty Chicken Burgers (page 51) always guaranteed clean plates at home; so much so, I would often cook 16 burgers at a time and plan to freeze them for another day only to find they are all gone.

It's a great idea to make more than you need, covering yourself for those busy days. I like to have a list on my freezer that I update whenever I put in or take out a dish. This way, meals don't get forgotten.

I'm a big fan of planning ahead, so I've dedicated a chapter (Prepare Ahead) to my best teatime triumphs, which have been prepared in advance and frozen. You don't have to be superwoman to serve up my Tuna Tagliatelle Bake (page 132) with a little help from a can of cream of tomato soup, Easy Beef Casserole (page 119) or Multi-layered Cottage Pie (page 129) on a school night. The trick is simple ingredients and an easy-to-follow cooking method. Good, wholesome meals needn't be expensive either; frozen fruit and vegetables can be cheaper than fresh, but just as nutritious. Dried and canned lentils and beans are also great as they're full of goodness, ideal for bulking up meals and inexpensive.

Weekends are the ideal time for planning ahead and filling up the freezer with midweek meals. It also offers the perfect opportunity to extend the dining table, dust down the emergency chairs and invite family and friends over. I enjoy nothing more than welcoming over my nearest and dearest friends and family and cooking up meals that everyone will enjoy tucking into such as my Perfect Paella (page 170) or Roast Leg of Lamb (page 149) with all the trimmings.

My secret to feeding extra mouths is to keep the menu simple. That doesn't mean you can't be a little adventurous, but don't put unnecessary pressure on yourself. Most of the recipes in my Weekend chapter can be easily halved or doubled depending on how many of you there are.

When I go to family or friend's houses, I always look forward to dessert. A surefire way to keep your guests sweet is my Peach, Apple & Raspberry Crumble (page 195), my Easy Chocolate and Orange Mousse (page 203) and my delicious Tiramisu (page 206), which are all very quick to prepare and use easy-to-find ingredients. For more feel-good puds flick to my collection of cakes and try my wonderful Chocolate Coffee Cake (page 186). It's good to bake a few fun treats now and then, and I believe they taste even more satisfying when they are the result of a family effort!

From around three years old, I got my children to help me in the kitchen – mixing, stirring, rolling dough and cutting out shapes. I also introduced a variety of foods too – this helped them understand the balance between healthy, wholesome foods and occasional treats. Once they had mastered the basics, I would let them have free reign of the kitchen every Friday to cook a meal for the family. Each month they would pick a recipe, and, as the weeks went on, they would get better at it. Believe me, we ate some intriguing dinners, but they had a lot of fun.

The weekend is a great time to get your children to help prepare food for their lunchboxes. It can be hard to come up with new ideas, week in, week out, so I've dedicated a chapter to Light Meals & Lunchboxes – quick-and-easy recipes that are perfect for the whole family. Here's a little tip; my secret weapon to getting children to eat pretty much anything is Annabel's Special Salad Dressing (page 86). In fact, my kids used to take a small bottle to school with them most days to share with their friends at lunch. Full of natural goodness and packed with flavour (and also great served with a salad as a first course when entertaining friends), I keep a bottle in my fridge at all times.

I hope that my cookbook of simple, delicious recipes brings you inspiration for lots of enjoyable family meals so you will never get stuck in a rut wondering what to make for dinner as you rush out the door to start your day. I would love for my family's favourite dishes to become your family's favourites too. Let my meals help you take the worry and stress out of everyday cooking.

Annabel X

Quick and easy

15-minute tomato sauce

Pesto and fresh basil transform an ordinary tomato sauce into something very special. You can vary the sauce by adding some sliced sautéed mushrooms, if you like.

PREP: 5 MINS
COOK: 15 MINS

225 g (8 oz) spaghettini
2 tbsp olive oil
1 small onion, finely chopped
1 garlic clove, crushed
¼–½ tsp finely chopped
    red chilli (optional)
2 × 400 g (14 oz) cans
    chopped tomatoes
2 tbsp red pesto
1 tsp balsamic vinegar
1 tsp caster sugar
1 tbsp chopped fresh basil
25 g (1 oz) Parmesan cheese,
    grated
salt and black pepper

1 Cook the spaghettini in a large saucepan of lightly salted water according to the packet instructions.

2 Meanwhile, heat the olive oil in a frying pan and sauté the onion, garlic and chilli (if using) for about 5 minutes.

3 Drain the juice from one of the cans of tomatoes and stir in the drained tomatoes and the second can of tomatoes and juice with all the other ingredients except the basil and Parmesan. Simmer for 10 minutes, then stir in the basil and Parmesan until melted. Season to taste before mixing with the cooked, drained spaghettini.

Penne with tuna and tomato sauce

MAKES 2-4 PORTIONS

Pasta is a good source of complex carbohydrates, which provide long-lasting energy. The red onion and sunblush tomatoes give this pasta dish a lovely flavour.

PREP: 5 MINS
COOK: 10 MINS

200 g (7 oz) penne
2 tbsp light olive oil
1 red onion, sliced
4 plum tomatoes, quartered, deseeded and roughly chopped
200 g (7 oz) can tuna in oil, drained
75 g (3 oz) sunblush tomatoes, chopped
1 tbsp balsamic vinegar
1 small handful fresh basil leaves, torn
salt and black pepper

1 Cook the penne in a large saucepan of lightly salted boiling water according to the packet instructions, then drain.

2 Heat the olive oil in a frying pan and sauté the onion for about 6 minutes, stirring occasionally until softened.

3 Stir in the fresh tomatoes and cook for 2–3 minutes until heated through and beginning to soften into the onions. Add the tuna, sunblush tomatoes, balsamic vinegar, basil and salt and pepper and heat for 1 minute before stirring into the pasta.

Bow-tie pasta with peas and prosciutto

MAKES 2-4 PORTIONS

Here is a simple and quick pasta dish that tends to be popular with young children. You could also add a little crème fraîche or double cream to the sauce if you like. The garlic is optional in this dish because it is especially pronounced; if you or your children aren't too keen on garlic, feel free to omit it.

PREP: 5 MINS
COOK: 15 MINS

1 tbsp olive oil
25 g (1 oz) butter
1 onion, finely chopped
1 garlic clove, crushed (optional)
75 g (3 oz) frozen peas
1 tbsp chopped fresh parsley
125 ml (4 fl oz) chicken stock
40 g (1½ oz) prosciutto,
    finely diced
200 g (7 oz) bow-tie pasta
2 tbsp freshly grated Parmesan
    cheese, plus extra to garnish
salt and black pepper

1 Heat the olive oil and a small knob of the butter in a frying pan and sauté the onion and garlic (if using) for about 8 minutes or until softened. Add the peas, cook for 1 minute, then stir in the parsley and chicken stock. Bring to the boil, then reduce the heat and cook for 4–5 minutes. Stir in the prosciutto.

2 Meanwhile, cook the pasta in a large saucepan of lightly salted water according to the packet instructions. Drain the pasta, return to the warm pan, add the remaining butter and toss until it melts. Stir in the grated Parmesan and season to taste. Reheat the peas and prosciutto and toss with the cooked pasta. Serve with some extra freshly grated Parmesan cheese if you wish.

Vegetable fusilli

MAKES 2-4 PORTIONS

A quick and tasty vegetable dish made with my special light cheese sauce, which couldn't be easier to prepare. Simply mix together vegetable stock, crème fraîche and Parmesan.

PREP: 8 MINS
COOK: 12 MINS

200 g (7 oz) fusilli pasta
   (or similar)
100 g (4 oz) small broccoli florets
75 g (3 oz) frozen peas
15 g (½ oz) butter
1 onion, finely chopped
1 garlic clove, crushed
250 ml (8fl oz) vegetable stock
6 tbsp full-fat crème fraîche
4 tomatoes, deseeded and diced
75g (3 oz) Parmesan cheese,
   grated
salt and black pepper

1 Cook the pasta in a large saucepan of lightly salted water according to the packet instructions. Add the broccoli and peas 4 minutes before the end of the cooking time. Drain.

2 Melt the butter in a large frying pan or wok and sauté the onion for 5 minutes until soft. Add the garlic and sauté for 1 minute, then add the stock and bring to the boil. Add the cooked pasta, vegetables, crème fraîche, tomatoes and Parmesan. Season to taste with salt and pepper, then toss everything together over the heat for 1–2 minutes before serving.

Tasty 10-minute prawn stir-fry

MAKES 4 PORTIONS

Here is a tasty stir-fry with colourful crunchy vegetables and carrot curls, which is very quick to prepare. Serve with boiled rice, if you like.

PREP: 10 MINS
COOK: 10 MINS
100 g (4 oz) baby sweetcorn
100 g (4 oz) carrots
1½ tbsp vegetable oil
2 spring onions, chopped
100 g (4 oz) green beans, trimmed
250 ml (8 fl oz) chicken stock
1 tbsp soy sauce
2 tbsp sake (rice wine) or sherry
2 tbsp cornflour
225 g (8 oz) cooked king prawns

1 Halve the sweetcorn lengthways and cut the carrots into thin batons. Heat the oil in a wok or frying pan and sauté the spring onions for 1 minute. Add the other vegetables and stir-fry for 2–3 minutes. Remove the vegetables and set aside.

2 Mix together the chicken stock, soy sauce, sake or sherry and cornflour. Pour the mixture into the wok and stir constantly while bringing to the boil. Reduce the heat and simmer, stirring, for 1–2 minutes until thickened. Stir in the prawns and the vegetables and heat through before serving.

Posh fish fingers

MAKES 4 PORTIONS

Crushed cornflakes make a delicious coating for fried fish. Serve these
crispy fingers with oven-baked chips and fresh lemon wedges for squeezing.
I also like to serve them with a cherry tomato and mozzarella salad.
I make the dressing by mixing 3 tablespoons olive oil with 1 tablespoon
balsamic vinegar, 1 tablespoon soy sauce and ½ teaspoon caster sugar.

PREP: 10 MINS
COOK: 10 MINS

400 g (14 oz) lemon sole, cod,
   plaice or hake fillets, skinned
85 g (3½ oz) cornflakes
30 g (1¼ oz) freshly grated
   Parmesan cheese
100g plain flour
2 medium eggs, lightly beaten
4 tbsp sunflower oil, for frying
salt and black pepper

1 Cut the fish into strips. Put the cornflakes into
a food processor and blitz, then pour into a bowl
and mix together with the Parmesan. Put the
flour into a bowl and season with salt and pepper.
Beat the eggs in another bowl. Now dip each piece
of fish in the flour, then the eggs and finally
the cornflake and Parmesan mixture.

2 Heat 2 tablespoons of the oil in a large frying
pan. Fry half the fish for 4–5 minutes, turning
them regularly until they are cooked. Drain on
kitchen paper. Add the remaining 2 tablespoons
of oil to the pan and cook the second batch of fish.
Drain as before, then serve with chips or salad
and lemon wedges, if you like.

Stir-fried chicken with broccoli

MAKES 4 PORTIONS

Stir-frying in a wok is a quick and easy method of cooking. Children tend to like Chinese food so making easy versions in your own kitchen can encourage children to enjoy eating vegetables. It is good to introduce new vegetables like shiitake mushrooms, which have a lovely subtle flavour.

PREP: 10 MINS
COOK: 10 MINS

2 skinless chicken breasts, cut into strips or chunks
1 tbsp sake (rice wine)
½ tbsp cornflour
2½ tbsp vegetable oil
1 garlic clove, crushed
1 onion, thinly sliced
1 medium carrot, peeled and cut into matchsticks
175 g (6 oz) broccoli, cut into small florets
75 g (3 oz) shiitake mushrooms, finely sliced
100 ml (3½fl oz) chicken stock
1 tbsp oyster sauce
½ tsp caster sugar
salt and black pepper

1 Season the strips of chicken with a little salt. Mix together the sake and cornflour, toss with the strips of chicken and set aside.

2 Heat 1 tablespoon of the oil in a wok, add half the garlic and the chicken and stir-fry for 2 minutes. Remove the chicken to a bowl and set aside.

3 Heat the remaining oil, add the remaining garlic, the onion and carrot and stir-fry for 3 minutes. Add the broccoli and mushrooms and stir-fry for 4 minutes.

4 Mix together the chicken stock, oyster sauce and sugar. Return the chicken to the wok, add the sauce and stir-fry for 1 minute. Season to taste.

Chicken, tomato and basil pasta

MAKES 2-4 PORTIONS

A quick, easy pasta dish that can be made in just 20 minutes from
ingredients that can be picked up on the way home from work.

PREP: 10 MINS
COOK: 10 MINS

200 g (7 oz) fusilli pasta
2 tbsp olive oil
1 onion, chopped
2 garlic cloves, crushed
4 tomatoes, deseeded and diced
1 cooked skinless chicken
    breast, diced
150 ml (5 fl oz) chicken stock
3 tbsp chopped fresh basil
1 tsp balsamic vinegar
50 g (2 oz) Parmesan cheese,
    grated
salt and black pepper

1 Cook the pasta in a large saucepan of lightly salted
water according to the packet instructions, then drain.

2 Heat the oil in another saucepan. Add the onion
and fry until soft. Add the garlic and tomatoes
and fry for about 1 minute. Add the chicken, stock,
basil, balsamic vinegar and stir in the drained pasta.
Season to taste with salt and black pepper. Toss
over the heat then remove from the heat and
add the Parmesan.

Jewelled couscous salad

MAKES 4 PORTIONS

The caramelised pecans and dried cranberries
add a delicious, sweet flavour to this salad.

**PREP: 10 MINS,
PLUS SOAKING
COOK: 5 MINS**

180 g (6½ oz) couscous
300 ml (10 fl oz) hot vegetable
    stock
1 red pepper, deseeded and diced
1 bunch spring onions, sliced
1 bunch fresh parsley, chopped
50 g (2 oz) dried cranberries,
    chopped
25 g (1 oz) butter
75 g (3 oz) pecans
25 g (1 oz) light soft brown sugar
salt and black pepper

For the dressing
1½ tbsp balsamic vinegar
1 tbsp white wine vinegar
1 tsp caster sugar
1 tsp Dijon mustard
6 tbsp olive oil

1 Measure the couscous into a bowl. Pour over the hot stock, stir, then cover with clingfilm and leave to soak for 20 minutes. Fluff up with a fork. Add the red pepper, spring onions, parsley, cranberries and season.

2 Mix all the dressing ingredients together and pour over the couscous.

3 Melt the butter in a small frying pan. Add the pecans, sprinkle over the sugar and cook over a fairly high heat to caramelise the nuts. Tip out of the pan, spread out and leave to cool, then roughly chop. Add to the couscous salad and mix together.

Potato and chicken rösti

MAKES 4 PORTIONS

The key to making a good rösti is to squeeze out as much moisture
from the potato (and carrots in the veggie version overleaf) as you can,
once it is grated. This will help the rösti hold its shape better.

PREP: 15 MINS
COOK: 12 MINS

200 g (7 oz) potato, grated
6 spring onions, sliced
75 g (3 oz) cooked chicken, diced
50 g (2 oz) frozen peas
25 g (1 oz) Parmesan cheese,
  grated
1 large egg, beaten
1 tbsp plain flour
A little vegetable oil and
  a knob of butter
salt and black pepper

1 Put the grated potato into a clean tea towel and squeeze
out the liquid. Put all the other ingredients into a bowl
and season well.

2 Heat 1 tablespoon of vegetable oil and the butter in
a small 20 cm (8 in) frying pan. Add the potato mixture
and flatten out. Fry for 5 minutes until lightly golden.
Put a large plate over the rösti in the frying pan, turn the
pan upside down so that the rösti is on the plate cooked
side up. Heat another 1 tablespoon of oil in the pan. Slide
the rösti back into the pan to cook on the other side for
about 7 minutes until cooked through. Cut into wedges
and serve.

Carrot and potato rösti

MAKES 4 PORTIONS

A simple rösti with well-seasoned, grated potato fried until golden and crunchy is hard to beat. Try my tasty veggie variation with grated potato, carrot, spring onions and peas.

PREP: 10 MINS
COOK: 12 MINS
225 g (8 oz) potatoes, peeled
125 g (4½ oz) carrot, peeled
1 medium egg, beaten
1 tbsp plain flour
6 spring onions, sliced
40 g (1½ oz) frozen peas
2 tbsp olive oil
salt and black pepper

1 Coarsely grate the potatoes and carrot into a clean tea towel and squeeze out as much liquid as you can. Put the vegetables into a bowl. Add the egg, flour, spring onions and peas, season well and mix together.

2 Heat the oil in a small 20 cm (8 in) frying pan. Add the mixture and press down gently to flatten. Fry for about 5 minutes until golden. Put a large plate over the rösti in the frying pan and turn the pan upside down so that the rösti is on the plate cooked side up. Slide the rösti back into the pan to fry the other side for another 5–7 minutes until cooked through. Cut into wedges and serve.

Tomato, sweet pepper and salami pasta

MAKES 2-4 PORTIONS

This pasta dish is a great favourite with children. You could also use sliced sausage instead of salami if you prefer.

PREP: 10 MINS
COOK: 20 MINS

1 tbsp olive oil
2 shallots, finely chopped
½ small red pepper, deseeded and chopped
400 g (14 oz) can chopped tomatoes, drained
180 ml (6 fl oz) strong chicken stock
225 g (8 oz) fusilli
1 tbsp chopped fresh basil
1 tbsp freshly grated Parmesan cheese
100 g (4 oz) salami, cut into strips
salt and black pepper

1 Heat the olive oil in a saucepan and sauté the shallots and red pepper for about 5 minutes or until softened. Stir in the tomatoes and sauté for 2 minutes, then add the stock and simmer for about 10 minutes.

2 Meanwhile, cook the pasta in a large saucepan of lightly salted water according to the packet instructions.

3 When the sauce is cooked, stir in the basil, Parmesan and salami. Heat through and season to taste. Drain the pasta and toss with the sauce.

Chicken schnitzel

I like to mix breadcrumbs with fresh herbs and Parmesan to make these
tasty schnitzels. Serve with a simple cucumber and fresh dill salad.

PREP: 12 MINS
COOK: 5 MINS
2 skinless chicken breasts
50 g (2 oz) plain flour
2 medium eggs, beaten
100 g (4 oz) white bread
1½ tbsp chopped fresh thyme
2 tbsp chopped fresh parsley
30 g (1¼ oz) Parmesan cheese,
   grated
A little vegetable oil and
   a knob of butter
salt and black pepper

For the cucumber and dill salad
1 cucumber
1½ tbsp freshly chopped dill
1 tbsp soy sauce
1 tbsp rice wine vinegar
1 tbsp mirin
2 tbsp light olive oil

1 Put the chicken on a board and cover with clingfilm.
Bash out using a rolling pin until very thin. Slice each
breast in half.

2 Put the flour in a shallow bowl. Put the eggs in
a separate bowl. Toss the chicken in the flour and
then dip in the egg and season.

3 Tear the bread into pieces and put it in a food
processor together with the herbs and Parmesan.
Whiz until it forms crumbs. Tip onto a plate and
coat the chicken in the crumbs.

4 Heat a large frying pan. Add a little vegetable oil and
the butter. Fry the chicken for 3–4 minutes on each side.

5 Meanwhile make the salad: top and tail the cucumber,
slice in half lengthways, then thinly slice into half moon
shapes. Put the cucumber into a bowl with the chopped
dill. Mix all the dressing ingredients together and pour
over the salad. Serve the hot schnitzels alongside a little
cool cucumber salad and lemon wedges.

Quick and easy prawn pasta bows

MAKES 4 PORTIONS

Bow-tie pasta always looks so appealing and you can rustle up
this dish in less than 15 minutes – perfect for school nights.

PREP: 10 MINS
COOK: 15 MINS
200 g (7 oz) bow-tie pasta
50 g (2 oz) frozen peas
2 tbsp olive oil
1 onion, chopped
1 red pepper, deseeded and diced
2 garlic cloves, crushed
300 ml (10 fl oz) chicken stock
1 tsp rice wine vinegar
2½ tsp soy sauce
2 tsp caster sugar
2 tsp cornflour
knob of butter
325 g (11 oz) raw king prawns,
  shelled
30 g (1¼ oz) Parmesan cheese,
  grated
salt and black pepper

1 Cook the pasta in a large saucepan of lightly salted
water according to the packet instructions. Add the
peas for the final 3 minutes of cooking before draining.

2 Meanwhile, heat the oil in another saucepan. Add the
onion and red pepper and fry for 8 minutes until just
soft. Add the garlic and fry for 30 seconds. Add the stock,
vinegar, soy sauce and sugar. Bring to the boil. Whisk
the cornflour with 1 tablespoon of cold water. Add to
the sauce and stir to thicken.

3 Melt the butter in a frying pan. Add the prawns and
fry until pink and cooked through.

4 Drain the pasta and peas and add them to the sauce
with the prawns. Toss together and season to taste.
Stir in the Parmesan and serve.

Easy bolognese sauce

MAKES 4 ADULT OR 8 CHILD PORTIONS

This is a quick and easy way to make a bolognese sauce using a can of tomato soup as one of the ingredients. Since red meat provides the best source of iron, it's good to find some family favourites that include it and this sauce is particularly appealing to children.

PREP: 10 MINS
COOK: 20 MINS
1 tbsp vegetable oil
1 large onion, chopped
1 garlic clove, crushed
500 g (1 lb 2 oz) lean minced beef
½ tsp mixed freeze-dried herbs
100 g (4 oz) button mushrooms, sliced
400 g (14 oz) can chopped tomatoes
1 × 295 g (10 oz) can condensed cream of tomato soup
400 g (14 oz) spaghetti
salt and black pepper

1 Heat the oil in a saucepan and sauté the onion and garlic for 2–3 minutes. Add the beef and the herbs and sauté until the beef has changed colour. Add the sliced mushrooms and sauté for 2 minutes. Add the remaining ingredients and cook over a medium heat for about 15 minutes. Season to taste.

2 Meanwhile, cook the spaghetti in a large saucepan of lightly salted water according to the packet instructions, then drain. Mix the cooked pasta with the bolognese sauce and serve.

Steak with tarragon and mushroom sauce

MAKES 4 PORTIONS

A quick-and-easy sauce that turns a simple steak into something very special.

PREP: 10 MINS
COOK: 12 MINS

4 thick sirloin or fillet steaks
3 tbsp olive oil
1 small onion, chopped
1 garlic clove, crushed
150 ml (5 fl oz) wine
100 ml (3½ fl oz) double cream
150 g (5 oz) brown mushrooms, sliced
a few drops Worcestershire sauce
1 tbsp chopped fresh tarragon
salt and black pepper

1 Take the steaks out of the fridge for 10 minutes before cooking. Season and rub with 2 tablespoons of olive oil. Heat a frying pan until hot. Fry the steaks for 4 minutes on each side until medium pink. Set aside on a plate to rest.

2 Heat the remaining olive oil in the pan. Add the onion and garlic and fry until soft. Add the wine and reduce by half. Add the cream and mushrooms. Stir for 3 minutes then add the Worcestershire sauce and tarragon and season. Serve the sauce with the rested steaks.

Pork stir-fry with sugar snap peas

MAKES 4 PORTIONS

A speedy stir-fry for busy weeknights. This dish can be made with pork or chicken – both will taste delicious.

PREP: 10 MINS
COOK: 12 MINS

300 g (11 oz) pork fillet or chicken breast, sliced into strips
1 tbsp honey
3 tbsp sunflower oil
6 spring onions, sliced
½ red chilli, deseeded and diced
200 g (7 oz) sugar snap peas
1 red pepper, deseeded and sliced
250 g (9 oz) brown mushrooms, halved
salt and black pepper

For the sauce
3 tbsp soy sauce
3 tbsp apple juice
1 tbsp rice wine vinegar
1 tbsp caster sugar
1 garlic clove, crushed
2 tsp cornflour

1 Toss the pork or chicken in the honey and season. Heat a frying pan until hot. Add 1 tablespoon of the oil and quickly brown the meat. Set aside.

2 Heat the remaining oil in the pan. Add the spring onions and chilli and fry for 1 minute. Add the remaining vegetables and stir-fry for 4–5 minutes.

3 Mix all the sauce ingredients together in a bowl.

4 Return the meat to the pan with the sauce. Toss everything together and fry for 2–3 minutes.

Sesame beef stir-fry

MAKES 4 PORTIONS

Provided you are not vegetarian, it is important to include red meat in your child's diet, as red meat provides the richest source of iron. This recipe is a firm family favourite in my house. I usually make it using tail fillet cut into thin strips, which is slightly cheaper but has exactly the same taste and soft texture of proper fillet steak.

PREP: 10 MINS
COOK: 10–12 MINS

300 g (10 oz) beef fillet or rump
    steak, cut into very fine strips
1 tbsp honey
1½ tbsp sunflower oil
1 tbsp sesame oil
1 garlic clove, crushed
1 medium carrot, cut into
    matchsticks
100 g (4 oz) baby corn,
    cut into quarters
1 courgette (about 100 g/4 oz),
    cut into matchsticks
1 tbsp cornflour
150 ml (5 fl oz) beef stock
2 tbsp dark soft brown sugar
2 tbsp soy sauce
a few drops Tabasco sauce
1 tbsp sesame seeds

1 Coat the beef in the honey. Heat the sunflower oil in a frying pan or wok and fry the beef, in batches, to brown, then set aside.

2 Heat the sesame oil in a wok and stir-fry the garlic, carrot, baby corn and courgette for 3–4 minutes. Return the beef to the pan. Mix the cornflour with 1 tablespoon of water and stir into the beef stock. Stir this into the pan together with the sugar, soy sauce, Tabasco and sesame seeds. Bring to a simmer and cook until slightly thickened. Serve with plain boiled or steamed rice.

Everyday meals

Sautéed fish with courgettes and red pepper

MAKES 2 PORTIONS

It's a shame that for many children the only fish that they enjoy eating is fish fingers. However, this is a very tasty fish recipe that I have invented for children although it's also delicious for the whole family and may well tempt even the most reluctant fish eater.

**PREP: 15 MINS, PLUS
MARINATING TIME
COOK: 15–18 MINS**
350 g (12 oz) plaice, sole or cod
   fillets skinned and cut into
   strips about 6.5 cm (2½ in) long
1 tbsp lemon juice
1 tbsp chopped onion
3 tbsp vegetable oil
100 g (4 oz) courgettes,
   cut into strips
50 g (2 oz) red pepper,
   deseeded and cut into strips
a little flour, for coating
salt and black pepper

For the sauce
250 ml (8 fl oz) chicken stock
2 tsp soy sauce
1 tsp sesame oil
1 tbsp caster sugar
1 tsp cider vinegar
1 tbsp cornflour
1 spring onion, finely sliced

1 Rinse the fish fillets and pat dry with kitchen paper. Mix together the lemon juice, 1 tablespoon of water and the chopped onion. Add the fish and leave to marinate for about 30 minutes.

2 To make the sauce, mix together the stock, soy sauce, sesame oil, sugar, vinegar and cornflour. Pour the sauce into a saucepan, bring to the boil and simmer, stirring, for 2–3 minutes until thickened and smooth. Stir in the spring onions.

3 Heat 1 tablespoon of the oil in a saucepan and sauté the courgette and red pepper for 4 minutes. Strain the marinade from the fish and discard (including the onion), coat the fish lightly in flour seasoned with salt and pepper. Heat the remaining oil in a pan and sauté the fish for 3 minutes on each side or until cooked. Add the vegetables, pour over the sauce and cook for 2 minutes.

Nasi goreng

MAKES 6 PORTIONS

This is a delicious Indonesian recipe flavoured
with peanuts and a mild curry sauce.

**PREP: 15 MINS, PLUS
MARINATING TIME
COOK: ABOUT 40 MINUTES**

2 skinless chicken breasts,
   cut into chunks

For the marinade
3 tbsp soy sauce
½ tbsp sesame oil
1 tbsp dark soft brown sugar

1 tbsp sesame oil
1 large onion, finely chopped
2 tsp mild curry powder
½ tsp turmeric
350 g (12 oz) long-grain rice
900 ml (1½ pints) chicken stock
2 tbsp vegetable oil
3 spring onions, finely sliced
1 red pepper, deseeded and
   finely chopped
90 g (3½ oz) baby corn,
   cut into pieces
100 g (4 oz) frozen peas
1 tbsp molasses or dark soft
   brown sugar
50 g (2 oz) roasted peanuts,
   finely chopped

1 Mix up the marinade and add the chicken pieces.
Leave to marinate in the fridge for at least 1 hour.
Remove the chicken and set the marinade to one side.

2 Heat 1 tablespoon of sesame oil in a large saucepan
and sauté the onion, curry powder and turmeric for
4 minutes. Add the rice and cook for 1 minute, stirring
to make sure that all the grains are coated. Pour in the
stock and simmer for about 20 minutes or until the
rice is tender. Drain the rice and set aside.

3 Meanwhile, in a wok or frying pan, heat the vegetable
oil and fry the chicken for about 3 minutes or until
sealed. Add the spring onions, red pepper and baby
corn and pour over the soy sauce from the marinade.
Cook the vegetables for 2–3 minutes. Add the frozen
peas and cook for a further 4 minutes. Add the rice
and stir in the molasses or dark soft brown sugar
and, finally, the chopped peanuts. Simmer for a few
minutes to heat through.

Tasty chicken burgers

MAKES 16 BURGERS

A great favourite in my house; my kids and their friends usually devour the lot so there are none left for me! Combining minced chicken with leek, onion, carrots and courgette keeps it super moist and very tasty. You can buy ready minced chicken or use a mix of breast and thigh meat and chop it in a food processor.

PREP: 15 MINS
COOK: 15–20 MINS

50 g (2 oz) finely chopped leek
1 onion, finely chopped
175 g (6 oz) carrots,
    peeled and grated
3½ tbsp sunflower oil, for frying
175 g (6 oz) courgettes, grated
500 g (1 lb 2 oz) minced chicken
    (breast and thigh)
1 apple, peeled, cored and grated
1 chicken stock cube,
    finely crumbled
175 g (6 oz) white breadcrumbs
salt and black pepper
a little flour, for dusting

1 Preheat the oven to 180°C/350°F/Gas 4.

2 Heat 1½ tablespoons of the oil in a frying pan and sauté the leek, onion and carrots for 3 minutes. Mix together with the remaining ingredients and chop in a food processor for a few seconds. Form the mixture into 16 burgers using floured hands.

3 Heat the remaining 2 tablespoons of oil in the frying pan and sauté the burgers for a few minutes each side until golden, then cook in the oven for 10–15 minutes.

Chicken fingers with curry dip

MAKES 3-4 PORTIONS

Chicken fingers are always popular but instead of tomato ketchup try
making this tasty mild curry dip… it only takes a few minutes to prepare.

PREP: 15 MINS
COOK: 20 MINS
4 slices white bread
3 large chicken breasts
a little plain flour, for coating
2 medium eggs, beaten
oil, for frying
salt and black pepper

Fot the sauce
1 tbsp olive oil
1 onion, chopped
1 garlic clove, crushed
1 large apple, peeled,
　cored and grated
1½ tsp curry paste
1 tsp plain flour
300 ml (10 fl oz) chicken stock
1 tbsp tomato ketchup
　or mango chutney
1½ tsp soy sauce

1 Put the bread into a food processor and whizz until
it forms breadcrumbs. Slice the chicken breasts into
goujon strips. Season and dip in the flour, then in the
egg, then coat in the breadcrumbs. Heat a little oil in
a frying pan and fry the fingers for about 5 minutes
on each side.

2 Make the sauce: heat the oil in a saucepan, add
the onion, garlic and apple and fry for 5 minutes
until soft. Add the curry paste and flour, then stir
in the stock, ketchup (or mango chutney) and soy
sauce. Bring to the boil and simmer for 2 minutes.
Transfer to a food processor or use an electric hand
blender to blend until smooth. Serve the sauce
as a dip for the chicken fingers.

Beef enchiladas

MAKES 6 PORTIONS

Tex-Mex enchiladas make a fun and tasty meal for the whole family.
I use sweet Spanish smoked paprika to add a subtle smoky flavour.

PREP: 10 MINS
COOK: ABOUT 40 MINS

1 tbsp olive oil
1 red onion, finely chopped
2 garlic cloves, crushed
1 red chilli, deseeded and
   finely chopped
500 g (1lb 2 oz) lean minced beef
2 tsp sweet Spanish smoked
   paprika
2 tsp ground coriander
2 tsp ground cumin
150 g (5 oz) brown mushrooms,
   sliced
100 g (4 oz) roasted red peppers
   (from a jar), chopped
150 ml (5 fl oz) beef stock
3 tbsp sundried tomato paste
6 small tortilla wraps
75 g (3 oz) Cheddar cheese, grated
400 g (14 oz) can chopped
   tomatoes
½ bunch fresh basil, chopped

1 Heat the olive oil in a saucepan. Add the onion, garlic and chilli and fry for 5 minutes until soft. Add the minced beef and fry until browned. Add the spices, mushrooms and peppers and fry for 2 minutes. Add the stock, cover with a lid and simmer for 20 minutes until tender. Add 1 tablespoon of the sundried tomato paste.

2 Preheat the grill. Warm the tortillas in the microwave. Divide the minced beef between the wraps. Sprinkle with half of the cheese. Roll up and place in a shallow ovenproof dish side by side.

3 Mix the chopped tomatoes, basil and remaining sundried tomato paste together. Spoon over the wraps and sprinkle with the remaining cheese. Place under the hot grill for 10 minutes until bubbling.

Teriyaki chicken skewers

MAKES 10 SKEWERS

If you like you can intersperse the chicken pieces with some chopped red onion and sweet pepper. You can also brush the vegetables with the marinade.

PREP: 10 MINS,
PLUS MARINATING
COOK: 20 MINS

3 tbsp soy sauce
2 tbsp rice wine vinegar
2 tbsp soft brown sugar
1 tbsp sesame oil
4 skinless chicken thighs
10 wooden skewers

1 Preheat the oven to 220°C/425°F/Gas 7.

2 Put the soy sauce, vinegar, sugar and oil into a dish. Slice the chicken into bite-sized cubes and marinate in the soy mixture for as long as possible.

3 Meanwhile, soak the wooden skewers in water for 10 minutes. Drain the chicken from the marinade (reserving the marinade for later). Thread the chicken onto the skewers. Place on a baking sheet and roast for 15–20 minutes until cooked through.

4 Put the reserved marinade into a saucepan. Bring to the boil and boil for 1–2 minutes until reduced. Pour the sauce over the chicken skewers.

Chicken with summer vegetables

MAKES 3 PORTIONS

Tender pieces of chicken and courgettes simmered
in a Parmesan and cream sauce, then finished with tomatoes,
rocket and pine nuts makes a satisfying supper.

PREP: 10 MINS
COOK: 20–25 MINS

2 ½ tbsp olive oil
1 red onion, sliced
150 g (4 oz) baby courgettes,
   cut into batons
2 skinless chicken breasts,
   cut into about 6 pieces
100 ml (3½ fl oz) white wine
150 ml (5 fl oz) single cream
4 tbsp freshly grated Parmesan
   cheese
10 cherry tomatoes, halved
30 g (1¼ oz) rocket leaves
2 tbsp pine nuts, toasted
salt and black pepper

1 Heat 1½ tablespoons of the olive oil in a saucepan
and sauté the onion for 5–6 minutes. Add the courgettes
and cook for 3–4 minutes until tender.

2 Season the chicken pieces with salt and pepper, heat
the remaining tablespoon of olive oil in a separate frying
pan and fry the chicken for about 6–7 minutes, turning
halfway through.

3 Add the wine to the courgettes and onion and boil
until reduced by half. Add the cooked chicken, cream
and Parmesan and simmer for about 1 minute. Stir
in the tomatoes and heat for a further minute, then
finally stir in the rocket and pine nuts and season
with salt and pepper.

Salmon fish cakes

MAKES 10 SMALL CAKES

The beauty of these fish cakes is that the salmon remains lovely and moist as you only need to cook them for about 5 minutes. The sweet chilli sauce, ketchup and grated Cheddar gives them a lovely flavour. You can keep the mixture in the fridge overnight if you don't want to make them all on the same day.

PREP: 10 MINS
COOK: 10 MINS

1 potato, weighing about
    250 g (9 oz)
4 spring onions, chopped
250 g (9 oz) salmon fillets, cubed
50 g (2 oz) Cheddar cheese, grated
1 tbsp tomato ketchup
2 tsp sweet chilli sauce
1 tsp lemon juice
1 tsp chopped fresh chives
50 g (2 oz) Japanese breadcrumbs
vegetable oil, for frying
salt and black pepper

1 Prick the potato with a fork. Cook the potato in the microwave for 10 minutes until soft. Scoop out the potato and mash with a fork. Put the spring onions, salmon and Cheddar into a food processor and whizz until coarsely chopped. Add to the potato with the ketchup, sweet chilli sauce, lemon juice and chives. Season and mix together. Shape into 10 rounds, then roll in the breadcrumbs.

2 Heat a little oil in a frying pan. Fry the fish cakes in 2 batches for about 5 minutes on each side until golden brown and cooked through. Drain on kitchen paper before serving.

Vegetable tagliatelle

MAKES 4 PORTIONS

As a variation you could add 250 g (9 oz) of cooked prawns
to the pasta. Add them with the stock and crème fraîche.

PREP: 10 MINS
COOK: 10–12 MINS

225 g (8 oz) tagliatelle
100g broccoli, cut into florets
50g French beans
2 tbsp olive oil
1 onion, finely chopped
1 garlic clove, crushed
1 small yellow pepper,
   deseeded and sliced
1 medium courgette, sliced
200 ml (7 fl oz) vegetable stock
125 g (4½ oz) full-fat
   crème fraîche
75 g (3 oz) Parmesan cheese,
   grated
10 cherry tomatoes, halved
2 tsp lemon juice
salt and black pepper

1 Cook the pasta in a large saucepan of lightly salted water according to the packet instructions. Add the broccoli and beans 3 minutes before the end of the cooking time. Drain.

2 Heat the olive oil in a frying pan. Add the onion and garlic and fry for 3 minutes. Add the yellow pepper and courgette and fry for 5–6 minutes until tender. Add the stock and crème fraîche and bring to the boil. Add the drained pasta and vegetables, Parmesan, tomatoes and lemon juice. Toss together and season well.

Tasty beef with rice

MAKES 4 PORTIONS

A simple recipe to turn minced beef into a tasty family meal.

PREP: 10 MINS
COOK: ABOUT 45 MINS
1 tbsp olive oil
1 onion, chopped
½ red pepper, deseeded and diced
1 carrot, diced
2 garlic cloves, crushed
300 g (11 oz) lean minced beef
400 g (14 oz) can chopped
   tomatoes
2 tbsp tomato purée
100 ml (3½ fl oz) apple juice
1 tbsp chopped fresh thyme
125 g (4½ oz) long-grain rice
50 g (2 oz) frozen peas
Parmesan cheese, for sprinkling
   (optional)
salt and black pepper

1 Heat the olive oil in a saucepan. Add the onion, red pepper and carrot and fry for 5 minutes. Add the garlic and beef and fry until browned. Add the tomatoes, purée, apple juice and thyme. Season and simmer, covered with a lid for 30 minutes until tender.

2 Cook the rice in a saucepan of boiling water according to the packet instructions. Add the peas 3 minutes before the end of the cooking time. Drain then mix the rice and peas with the mince. Sprinkle with Parmesan, if you like.

Minestrone

MAKES 8 PORTIONS

Minestrone is a family favourite in our house. Sometimes I leave out the baked beans and soup pasta and instead add a can of cartoon character pasta in tomato sauce, which seems to add to its nostalgic appeal.

PREP: 15 MINS
COOK: ABOUT 33 MINS

2 tbsp sunflower oil
1 onion, finely chopped
50 g (2 oz) leeks, diced
100 g (4 oz) carrots, diced
100 g (4 oz) potatoes,
   peeled and diced
100 g (4 oz) French beans, topped
   and tailed and cut into 12 mm
   (½ in) lengths
50 g (2 oz) celery, diced
1.8 litres (3 pints) chicken or
   vegetable stock
25 g (1 oz) tiny star-shaped pasta
100 g (4 oz) frozen peas or 100 g
   (4 oz) frozen baby broad beans
205 g (7 oz) can baked beans
salt and black pepper

1 Heat the oil in a large saucepan and sauté the onion and leeks for 2 minutes. Add the carrots, potatoes, French beans and celery and sauté for 4 minutes.

2 Add the chicken or vegetable stock and simmer, covered with a lid, for 15 minutes.

3 Add the pasta, peas or broad beans and the baked beans and continue to cook for 10 minutes. Season to taste and serve.

Turkey bolognese

MAKES 4 PORTIONS

This is a tasty, quick and easy sauce for pasta. You could
also make this using minced chicken as an alternative.

PREP: 10 MINS
COOK: ABOUT 35 MINS

2 tbsp vegetable oil
1 large onion, finely chopped
1 garlic clove, finely chopped
1 small red pepper, deseeded
  and finely diced
500 g (1 lb 2 oz) minced turkey
1 carrot, grated
400 g (14 oz) can chopped
  tomatoes
1 chicken stock cube dissolved
  in 150 ml (5 fl oz) boiling water
1 tbsp tomato ketchup
1 tbsp chopped fresh sage
  or ½ tsp dried sage
½ tbsp fresh thyme leaves
  or ¼ tsp dried thyme
350 g (12 oz) spaghetti or penne
salt and black pepper

1 Heat the oil in a saucepan and sauté the onion, garlic
and red pepper for 3–4 minutes. Add the minced turkey
and stir until it changes colour, breaking up any lumps
with a fork. Add the remaining ingredients, except
the pasta, bring to the boil then simmer, uncovered,
stirring occasionally, for 30 minutes.

2 Meanwhile, cook the pasta in a large saucepan of
lightly salted water according to the packet instructions.
Drain and toss with the sauce.

Crispy beef stir-fry

MAKES 4 PORTIONS

This beef stir fry has a lovely, rich flavour. Its important
to fry the beef in batches, otherwise the oil temperature will
decrease and the beef will stew instead of brown.

PREP: 10 MINS
COOK: 12–15 MINS

100 g (4 oz) egg noodles
1 medium egg
2 tbsp cornflour
225 g (8 oz) sirloin thin
   cut steaks
sunflower oil, for frying
½ red onion, sliced
2 small carrots, cut into
   matchsticks
½ red pepper, deseeded
   and sliced
1 garlic clove, crushed
2 tbsp rice wine vinegar
2 tsp soy sauce
1 tsp sesame oil
2 tbsp caster sugar
50 g (2 oz) beansprouts
salt and black pepper

1 Cook the noodles in boiling water according
to the packet instructions, until soft. Drain.

2 Mix the egg and cornflour together in a bowl.
Thinly slice the beef and season. Mix into the egg
mixture. Heat 2 cm (¾ in) of sunflower oil in a wok.
Once smoking, add the beef in two batches and
fry until crisp, for about 3–4 minutes, then drain
on kitchen paper.

3 Add more oil to the wok so that it is one-quarter
full then heat the oil. Add the onion, carrots and
red pepper and fry for 3 minutes. Add the garlic
and fry for about 30 seconds. Mix the vinegar, soy
sauce, sesame oil and sugar together. Add to the wok
with the noodles and beef, toss together and season.
Add the beansprouts and cook for 1 minute then
remove from the heat and serve.

Chicken satay skewers

MAKES 5 PORTIONS

A kid-friendly recipe that adults will love too – and so easy to make.

**PREP: 15 MINS,
PLUS SOAKING AND
MARINATING TIMES
COOK: ABOUT 15 MINS**
2 chicken breasts
10 bamboo skewers

For the marinade
small piece of fresh ginger
1 garlic clove
juice of 1 lime
1 tbsp soy sauce
1 tbsp runny honey
1 tsp peanut butter

For the sauce
100 g (4 oz) peanut butter
   (crunchy)
5 tbsp coconut milk
1 tbsp sweet chilli sauce
1 tsp soy sauce

1 Soak the skewers in water for 30 minutes to stop them from scorching when you grill them.

2 Mix the marinade. Peel and grate the ginger (you should have about ¼ teaspoon), crush the garlic and put in a bowl along with the lime juice (set 1 teaspoon of the lime juice aside for later use), soy sauce, honey and peanut butter and whisk together.

3 Put the chicken breasts into a sealable polythene bag or cover with clingfilm and use a mallet or rolling pin to bash the chicken breasts until they are about ½ cm (¼ in) thick. Slice each chicken breast into 5 strips, add to the marinade and leave to marinate for about 30 minutes.

4 While the chicken is marinating you can make the sauce. Put the peanut butter, coconut milk, 5 tablespoons of water, the sweet chilli sauce and soy sauce in a small saucepan. Warm gently, stirring constantly, until everything has melted. Simmer for 1–2 minutes until the sauce thickens. Remove from the heat, then stir in the leftover lime juice and set aside.

5 Preheat the grill to medium-high. Thread the chicken strips onto the soaked skewers and put on a foil-lined baking sheet. Grill each side for about 5 minutes or until the chicken is cooked through. Serve with the dipping sauce.

Chicken piccata

MAKES 2 PORTIONS

Here are tender breasts of chicken cooked in a delicious,
quick-and-easy-to-prepare Chinese-style sauce.

PREP: 15 MINS, PLUS
MARINATING TIME
COOK: ABOUT 12 MINS

2 boneless chicken breasts
1 tbsp lemon juice
1 tbsp finely chopped onion
a little flour, for coating
2 tbsp vegetable oil
salt and black pepper

For the sauce
250 ml (8 fl oz) chicken stock
2 tsp soy sauce
1 tsp sesame oil
1 tbsp sugar
1 tsp cider vinegar
1 tbsp cornflour
ground white pepper
1 spring onion, thinly sliced

1 Rinse the chicken and pat dry with kitchen paper.
Place the chicken breasts under a layer of clingfilm.
Using the flat side of a meat mallet, pound until quite
thin and cut each breast in half. Remove the clingfilm
and place the chicken in a shallow dish.

2 Mix together the lemon juice and 1 tablespoon
of water, add the chopped onion and the chicken
and leave to marinate for 30 minutes. Remove the
chicken pieces and discard the marinade. Dip
the chicken in a little flour seasoned with salt
and pepper.

3 Heat the oil in a frying pan or wok and sauté the
chicken for about 5 minutes on each side or until
lightly browned and cooked through.

4 Meanwhile, put all the ingredients for the sauce into
a saucepan and bring to the boil. Cook over a medium
heat, stirring, until thickened. Drain away any excess
oil from the pan in which the chicken was cooked, pour
the sauce over the cooked chicken and heat through.

Marinated beef with vegetables

MAKES 4–5 PORTIONS

This tasty and fast beef stir-fry makes a great all-in-one meal.

PREP: 20 MINS, PLUS
MARINATING TIME
COOK: ABOUT 25 MINS

225 g (8 oz) beef fillet, rump
  or sirloin cut into strips
175 g (6 oz) pasta twirls
100 g (4 oz) carrots, peeled
  and sliced or cut into stars
175 g (6 oz) new potatoes
100 g (4 oz) French beans,
  topped and tailed
3 tbsp sunflower oil
1 garlic clove, crushed
1 onion, thinly sliced
100 g (4 oz) red pepper,
  deseeded and cut into strips
salt and black pepper

For the marinade
1 tbsp soy sauce
1 tbsp sake or sherry
1 tsp sesame oil
1 tsp cornflour

For the sauce
½ chicken stock cube dissolved
  in 6 tbsp boiling water
½ tsp rice wine vinegar
1 tsp soy sauce
1 tsp caster sugar
½ tsp cornflour

1 Mix all the ingredients for the marinade together in a bowl and marinate the beef strips in the fridge for at least 20 minutes.

2 Cook the pasta in a large saucepan of lightly salted boiling water according to the packet instructions, drain, set aside and keep warm. Steam the carrots, potatoes and French beans for about 6 minutes or until tender.

3 Meanwhile, heat 1 tablespoon of the oil in a wok or frying pan and stir-fry the marinated beef for 3 minutes. Remove the beef from the wok and set aside.

4 In the same wok or pan, heat the remaining oil and sauté the garlic and onion for 3 minutes. Mix together all the ingredients for the sauce. Add the red pepper to the onion and cook for 2 minutes, cut the potatoes into slices and add these together with the carrots, French beans and beef and season with some salt and pepper. Stir in the sauce and cooked pasta and cook for 2 minutes.

Honeyed lamb cutlets

MAKES 6 LAMB CUTLETS

Children like eating food with their fingers, which is one reason
why lamb cutlets are popular. They are especially delicious if marinated
in honey and soy sauce first. Serve with Mashed potatoes with sweet
potato and carrots (page 79) and some green vegetables.

**PREP: 5 MINS, PLUS
MARINATING TIME
COOK: ABOUT 8 MINS**
6 lamb cutlets

For the marinade
2 tbsp soy sauce
1 tbsp runny honey
½ tsp sesame oil

1 Mix all the ingredients for the marinade together and
marinate the cutlets for at least 2 hours or overnight.

2 Preheat the grill to high. Cook the marinated cutlets
under the hot grill for about 8 minutes, turning halfway
through. Brush with the marinade during cooking.

Meatballs with sweet-and-sour sauce

MAKES 5 PORTIONS

These tasty meatballs in a sweet-and-sour sauce are a family favourite.
It is useful to keep a stock of these meatballs in the freezer.

PREP: 15 MINS
COOK: ABOUT 25 MINS
450 g (1 lb) lean minced beef
1 onion, finely chopped
1 apple, peeled, cored and grated
50 g (2 oz) fresh white
    breadcrumbs
1 tbsp chopped fresh parsley
1 chicken stock cube, finely
    crumbled
2 tbsp vegetable oil, for frying
salt and black pepper
a little flour, for dusting

For the sweet-and-sour sauce
1 tbsp soy sauce
½ tbsp cornflour
1 tbsp vegetable oil
1 onion, finely chopped
50 g (2 oz) red pepper,
    deseeded and chopped
400 g (14 oz) can chopped
    tomatoes
1 tbsp malt vinegar
1 tsp soft brown sugar

1 Mix together all the ingredients for the meatballs, apart from the vegetable oil, with 2 tablespoons of cold water, and chop for a few seconds in a food processor. Using floured hands, form into about 20 meatballs. Heat the oil in a frying pan and sauté the meatballs for about 10–12 minutes, turning occasionally, until browned and sealed.

2 Meanwhile, to make the sauce, mix together the soy sauce and cornflour in a small bowl. Heat the oil in a pan and sauté the onion for 3 minutes. Add the red pepper and sauté, stirring occasionally, for 2 minutes. Add the tomatoes, vinegar and sugar, season with pepper and simmer for 10 minutes. Add the soy sauce mixture and cook for 2 minutes, stirring occasionally. Blend using an electric hand blender then sieve or purée the sauce through a mouli.

3 Pour the sauce over the meatballs, cover and simmer for about 5 minutes or until cooked through.

Finger-licking chicken drumsticks

MAKES 4 PORTIONS

Chicken drumsticks tend to be very popular with children and are good either hot or cold. This tasty marinade gives them a wonderful flavour and they can be prepared the day before, refrigerated and then wrapped in foil for your child's lunchbox.

PREP: 10 MINS, PLUS MARINATING TIME
COOK: 35–40 MINS

4 large chicken drumsticks

For the marinade
1½ tbsp cider or white wine vinegar
4 tbsp tomato sauce
2 tbsp runny honey
½ tbsp mustard
½ tbsp Worcestershire sauce
½ tbsp vegetable oil

1 Mix all the ingredients for the marinade together in a bowl.

2 Skin the drumsticks, make 2 or 3 slashes in the flesh and add to the marinade, turning a few times to make sure that they are well coated. Cover and refrigerate for at least 2 hours or overnight.

3 Preheat the oven to 220°C/425°F/Gas 7.

4 Arrange the drumsticks in a shallow roasting tin and pour over the marinade. Cook for 35–40 minutes, or until cooked through, basting occasionally with the sauce.

Salmon teriyaki

MAKES 4 PORTIONS

It's well worth investing in a bottle of sake or sherry and mirin (a sweet Japanese cooking wine), as you will want to make this recipe over and over again.

PREP: 10 MINS, PLUS
MARINATING TIME
COOK: ABOUT 10 MINS

4 × 150 g (5 oz) thick fillets
  of salmon, skinned
2 tbsp vegetable oil
150 g (5 oz) button mushrooms,
  sliced
150 g (5 oz) beansprouts

For the marinade
1½ fl oz soy sauce
2 fl oz sake (rice wine)
  or sherry
1 fl oz mirin
1 tbsp caster sugar

1 Mix all the ingredients for the marinade together in a saucepan and stir over a medium heat until the sugar has dissolved. Take off the heat, add the salmon and marinate for 10 minutes.

2 Heat half the oil in a frying pan or wok and sauté the mushrooms for 2 minutes, then add the beansprouts and cook for a further 2 minutes.

3 Meanwhile, drain the salmon, reserving the marinade. Heat the remaining oil in a frying pan and sauté the salmon for 1–2 minutes on each side or until slightly browned. Pour away the excess oil from the frying pan. Alternatively, it is particularly good if you cook the salmon on a very hot griddle pan brushed with a little oil.

4 After 2 minutes of cooking pour a little of the teriyaki sauce over the salmon and cook for a few minutes, basting occasionally. Simmer the remaining teriyaki sauce in a small saucepan until thickened. Divide the vegetables between four plates, place the salmon on top and pour the teriyaki sauce over the fish. Serve with basmati rice.

Annabel's chicken goujons

MAKES 2 PORTIONS

These are simply the best chicken goujons! Marinating the chicken in the buttermilk mixture ensures the meat is very tender once cooked, and gives a great taste.

PREP: 20 MINS, PLUS
MARINATING TIME
COOK: ABOUT 8 MINS

200 ml (7 fl oz) buttermilk
1 tsp Worcestershire sauce
1 tsp soy sauce
¼ tsp paprika
1 garlic clove, sliced
300 g (11 oz) skinless chicken
   breast, cut into goujons
   (about 8 × 4 cm/7¼ × 1½ in)
100 g (4 oz) plain flour
1 large egg, beaten
115 g (4 oz) fine dried
   breadcrumbs
40 g (1½ oz) finely grated
   Parmesan cheese
sunflower oil, for frying
salt and black pepper

1 Mix the buttermilk, Worcestershire sauce, soy sauce, paprika and garlic together in a bowl. Add the chicken strips and toss to coat. Cover and marinate for at least 1 hour or overnight in the fridge.

2 Season the flour with a little salt and pepper and spread it out on a plate. Put the egg in a small, shallow bowl. On another plate, mix together the breadcrumbs and Parmesan.

3 Drain the chicken. Dip in the seasoned flour, then in the beaten egg and finally the breadcrumbs and cheese.

4 Heat the oil in a large frying pan and sauté the chicken for 2–2½ minutes on each side until golden and cooked through, turning occasionally. Drain on kitchen paper. Serve with a tomato relish and lemon wedges, if you like.

Chicken karmel

MAKES 4 PORTIONS

This sweet-and-sour chicken recipe is a great favourite with my family.
To make eating fun you can buy child-friendly plastic chopsticks that are joined
at the top so that they only need to be squeezed together to pick up food. This
recipe would be perfect for these as everything is cut into bite-sized pieces.

PREP: 15 MINS
COOK: 15 MINS
4 tbsp vegetable oil
250 g (9 oz) skinless
    chicken breasts, cut
    into bite-sized cubes
75 g (3 oz) carrot, cut into
    matchsticks
50 g (2 oz) baby corn,
    sliced in half lengthways
    then in half across
50 g (2 oz) fine green beans,
    topped and tailed and
    cut in half
2 spring onions, finely sliced
salt and black pepper

For the batter
1 medium egg yolk
1½ tbsp cornflour
1 tbsp milk

For the sweet-and-sour sauce
1 tbsp soy sauce
2 tbsp tomato ketchup
2 tbsp rice wine vinegar
2 tbsp caster sugar
½ tsp sesame oil

1 Make the batter: in a small bowl, beat together the
egg yolk, cornflour and milk to make a thin batter.
Heat 2 tablespoons of the oil in a wok, dip the chicken
into the batter, then fry for 3–4 minutes until golden.
Remove from the wok and set aside.

2 Meanwhile, mix together all the ingredients for
the sauce. Heat the remaining oil in a wok and stir-fry
the carrot, baby corn and green beans for 2 minutes.
Add the sauce, bring to the boil and cook for 2 minutes.
Remove from the heat and stir in the spring onions.
Add the chicken to the vegetables and heat through.
Season to taste. Serve with fluffy white rice.

Mashed potato with sweet potato and carrot

MAKES 4 PORTIONS

There are lots of different ways to turn ordinary mashed potato into something special. Mashed potato and sweet potato with milk, butter and a little grated Parmesan cheese is especially good.

PREP: 15 MINS
COOK: 18–22 MINS

450 g (1 lb) white potatoes, peeled
450 g (1 lb) sweet potatoes, peeled
3 carrots, peeled
150 ml (5 fl oz) milk
a knob of butter
50 g (2 oz) Parmesan cheese, grated
salt and black pepper

1 Slice the potatoes into cubes and cut the carrots into slices. Put into a saucepan and cover with water. Bring to the boil, then boil for 16–20 minutes until tender. Drain and mash. Add the milk, butter and Parmesan and stir until smooth. Season well.

Broccoli with chilli and pine nuts

MAKES 4–6 PORTIONS

Broccoli is king of superfoods – here is a way to spice it up.

PREP: 5 MINS
COOK: ABOUT 8 MINS
25 g (1 oz) pine nuts
400 g (14 oz) broccoli florets
2 tbsp olive oil
½ red chilli, deseeded and diced
1 garlic clove, crushed
2 tsp lemon juice
salt and black pepper

1 Heat a frying pan. Brown the pine nuts, stirring occasionally to make sure they don't burn and set aside.

2 Steam the broccoli for 2 minutes or cook it in a saucepan of boiling water for 2 minutes. Drain.

3 Heat the olive oil in the frying pan. Add the chilli and garlic and fry for 20 seconds. Add the broccoli and stir-fry for 2 minutes. Add the lemon juice and season.

Light meals, snacks and lunchboxes

Mini muffin pizzas

MAKES 4 MINI PIZZAS

These mini pizzas are delicious. I have used a courgette and cherry tomato topping but you can choose any topping, perhaps adding some diced ham on top of the tomato sauce before covering with grated cheese. Otherwise, just make a simple cheese and tomato pizza without any extra toppings. You can double the quantity of tomato sauce and keep it in the fridge ready for when you want to make pizzas. You can also make these using chilled pizza dough bought in the supermarket, which you simply roll out and cut into circles (following the instructions on the packet).

PREP: 10 MINS
COOK: 10 MINS
1 tbsp olive oil
½ small onion, finely chopped
  (about 50 g/2 oz)
1 small garlic clove, crushed
100 ml (3½ fl oz) passata
½ tbsp tomato purée
a pinch of caster sugar
1 tbsp chopped fresh basil
  leaves, (optional)
2 English muffins, halved
75 g (3 oz) grated Cheddar
  or mozzarella cheese,
  or a mixture of both
salt and black pepper

Toppings
courgettes
cherry tomatoes
sliced salami
pepperoni
diced ham and pineapple
sweetcorn
sweet pepper
mushrooms
sliced pitted olives
basil

1 Preheat the grill to high. Heat the olive oil in a small saucepan and sauté the onion and garlic for 3–4 minutes. Add the passata, together with the tomato purée and seasoning and cook for about 2 minutes or until the mixture is thick enough to spread. Remove from the heat and stir in the chopped basil (if using).

2 Toast the split muffins and divide the tomato sauce between them. Choose your favourite topping and then cover with the grated cheese. Place under the hot grill until golden and bubbling – about 2 minutes.

Annabel's special salad and dressing

MAKES 4 PORTIONS

My children go mad for this dressing and pour it over everything! They always preferred to come home to a bowl of salad with this dressing than a bag of crisps or a chocolate biscuit. I often serve this recipe as a first course when I'm entertaining and I'm always asked for the recipe, so here it is…

PREP: 15 MINS

a generous handful of pine nuts
200 g (7 oz) bag mixed salad
4 tomatoes cut into quarters
    (300 g/11 oz)
75 g (3 oz) fine green beans
198g (7 oz) can sweetcorn
1 avocado, peeled and chopped

For the dressing
25 g (1 oz) finely chopped onion
50 ml (2 fl oz) sunflower oil
2 tbsp rice wine vinegar
½ tbsp fresh chopped ginger root
1 tbsp chopped celery
1 tbsp soy sauce
1½ tsp tomato purée
1½ tsp caster sugar
salt and black pepper

1 To make the dressing, combine all the ingredients, except for the salt and pepper, with 2 tablespoons of water in a blender or food processor and whizz until smooth. Season to taste.

2 To make the salad, sauté the pine nuts in a dry frying pan until lightly golden. Mix together with all of the other salad ingredients and toss with the dressing.

Cheese, chive and tomato omelette

MAKES 1 PORTION

This is a delicious folded omelette, flavoured with chives and filled with fresh tomatoes and melted cheese. If you don't have any chives, then make a herb omelette using ¼ teaspoon mixed dried herbs instead.

PREP: 5 MINS
COOK: 5 MINS
2 large eggs
1 tbsp chives, snipped
a knob of butter
1 tomato, chopped
30 g (1¼ oz) grated Gruyere
   or Cheddar cheese
salt and black pepper

1 Beat the eggs with the chives and season with a little salt and pepper. Melt the butter in a 20 cm (8 in) frying pan, add the beaten eggs and chives and swirl the mixture around to coat the pan evenly.

2 When the edges of the egg begin to set, carefully lift the egg with a spatula, tilt the pan towards the edge you have lifted and let the uncooked egg flow underneath the cooked portion to cover the base of the pan.

3 Spoon the tomatoes and grated cheese on to one side of the omelette. Fold the omelette over and cook for about 1 minute over a gentle heat until the omelette is set and the cheese is melted.

Welsh rarebit

MAKES 2 PORTIONS

This is the perfect mixture for a really tasty Welsh Rarebit.
Traditionally Welsh Rarebit is flavoured with beer but you can use
milk instead. To make fresh breadcrumbs simply tear a slice of
white bread into pieces and whizz in a food processor.

PREP: 5 MINS
COOK: 5 MINS

150 g (5 oz) mature Cheddar
 cheese, grated
2 tbsp milk or beer
a few drops Worcestershire sauce
a generous pinch of dried
 mustard powder
1 medium egg yolk,
 lightly beaten
3 tbsp fresh white breadcrumbs
2 thick slices wholemeal
 or white bread
paprika, for sprinkling

1 Place the cheese and milk or beer in a saucepan
over a low heat, stirring until melted. Add the
Worcestershire sauce and mustard powder and
stir in. Remove from the heat and beat in the
egg yolk. Stir in the breadcrumbs.

2 Preheat the grill to high. Toast the slices of bread
and spread with the Rarebit topping, then sprinkle
with paprika. Cook the Rarebits under the grill for
about 2 minutes until golden and bubbling. Serve
with a watercress salad, if you like.

Sweetcorn and broccoli fritters

MAKES 12

Simply mix all the ingredients together and then drop the mixture into the pan to make tasty vegetable fritters. These fritters are best eaten straight away so that they stay crispy on the outside. You can store any extra mixture in the fridge and keep it for the next day.

PREP: 10 MINS
COOK: 15 MINS

150 g (5 oz) broccoli, cut into florets
150 g (5 oz) can sweetcorn, drained
150 g (5 oz) self-raising flour
1 medium egg, beaten
2 tbsp milk
2 tbsp chopped fresh basil leaves
2 tbsp sweet chilli sauce
75 g (3 oz) Cheddar cheese, grated
2 tbsp finely chopped spring onion
sunflower oil, for frying
salt and black pepper

1 Steam the broccoli florets for about 8 minutes, then chop into small pieces. Blitz the sweetcorn in a food processor. Mix all of the ingredients together, except the oil, and season to taste.

2 Heat the oil in a large frying pan. Drop spoonfuls of the mixture into the frying pan and fry for about 2 minutes on each side, or until golden. When cooked, transfer to a plate lined with kitchen paper. Serve warm with tzatziki, if you like.

Chicken pasta salad

MAKES 4 PORTIONS

A quick and easy salad that is very nutritious and great
for lunchboxes or a light snack. This has a tasty dressing
that children and grown ups will love!

PREP: 10 MINS
COOK: 12–15 MINS
110 g (4 oz) fusilli
100 g (4 oz) broccoli florets
100 g (4 oz) cooked chicken
   breast, chopped
100 g (4 oz) canned sweetcorn
10 cherry tomatoes, halved
4 spring onions, thinly sliced

For the dressing
3 tbsp light olive oil
1 tbsp rice wine vinegar
1 tsp caster sugar
½ tsp Dijon mustard
salt and black pepper

1 Cook the pasta in a saucepan of lightly salted boiling water according to the packet instructions, then drain. Steam the broccoli florets for 5 minutes. Meanwhile, whisk together the ingredients for the dressing.

2 Put the chopped chicken, sweetcorn, tomatoes and spring onions into a bowl together with the drained pasta and toss with the dressing.

Courgette fritters

MAKES 4 PORTIONS

If your children aren't keen on eating vegetables then
try these – they are delicious and were very popular with
my tasting panel – even the confirmed vegetable haters.

PREP: 10 MINS
COOK: 10 MINS
450 g (1 lb) courgettes
4 tbsp cornflour
8 tbsp plain flour
vegetable oil, for deep-frying
salt and black pepper

1 Wash and dry the courgettes and trim off the
ends. Cut them into sticks about 6 cm (2¼ in) long
and 2 cm (¾ in) wide and season them with salt
and pepper. Beat together 150 ml (5 fl oz) water,
the cornflour, plain flour and some salt and
pepper to form a thin batter.

2 Heat the oil in a deep-fat fryer with a basket filled
with oil to a depth of about 5 cm (2 in). Alternatively,
you could use a heavy saucepan and a metal slotted
spoon or strainer. Heat the oil until it reaches a
temperature of 190°C/375°F (you can tell when it is
hot enough for frying if a piece of vegetable sizzles
as it touches the oil). Dip the courgette sticks into
the batter and fry them for about 2 minutes or until
crispy and golden. Lift out the basket or remove the
courgette fritters with a slotted spoon or strainer.
Drain on kitchen paper and serve immediately.

Savoury breakfast muffins

MAKES 1 OR 2 PORTIONS

Cheese and tomato on toast makes a nutritious breakfast and using split toasted muffins makes a nice variation. You can vary the toppings depending on what you have on hand in the kitchen – try adding a slice of ham to each muffin too.

PREP: 5 MINS
COOK: 2–3 MINS
1 muffin (per person)
a little butter or margarine
1 thin slice of ham,
    cut in half (optional)
1 tomato, thinly sliced
50 g (2 oz) Cheddar cheese,
    grated
salt and black pepper

To garnish (optional)
2 cherry tomatoes
2 slices cucumber
1 black olive
1 slice of red pepper

1 Preheat the grill to high. Split and toast the muffin. Spread with a little butter or margarine. Arrange the ham, if using, over the muffin halves, then top with thinly sliced tomato. Lightly season and then cover with the grated cheese.

2 Place under the hot grill until lightly golden. If you wish, you can then have some fun decorating them to look like faces. Serve with the salad garnish, if you like.

Mango, apple and banana smoothie

MAKES 2 GLASSES

Look for a really sweet, ripe mango to make this summer smoothie.

PREP: 5 MINS
200 g (7 oz) chopped mango
75 g (3 oz) ripe banana,
    peeled and sliced
150 ml (5 fl oz) apple juice

1 Simply whizz all the ingredients together until smooth in an electric hand blender. Pour into 2 glasses.

Strawberry and peach smoothie

MAKES 2 GLASSES

To make a super chilled smoothie, freeze the banana already peeled in a plastic bag with the air pressed out before blending with the rest of the ingredients.

PREP: 5 MINS
100 g (4 oz) strawberries,
    hulled and cut into quarters
1 banana, peeled and sliced
    (can be frozen first)
1 large ripe peach,
    peeled, stoned and
    cut into pieces
150 ml (5 fl oz) low-fat
    strawberry drinking yogurt
125 ml (4 fl oz) freshly
    squeezed orange juice

1 Simply whizz all the ingredients together until smooth in an electric hand blender. Pour into 2 glasses.

Watermelon and strawberry refresher

MAKES 2 GLASSES

The perfect, fruity drink for a hot summer's day.

PREP: 5 MINS

400 g (14 oz) watermelon
   flesh, cut into cubes
150 g (5 oz) strawberries,
   hulled and cut in half
juice of 3 oranges
a little icing sugar, to sweeten

1 Simply whizz all the ingredients together in an electric hand blender and sweeten with a little icing sugar to taste.

Tomato, mozzarella and avocado salad

MAKES 2 PORTIONS OR 4 PORTIONS AS A SIDE SALAD

This is a slight twist on a traditional olive oil balsamic dressing as I add soy sauce, which gives this salad a delicious flavour.

PREP: 10 MINS

4 medium good-quality ripe tomatoes
150 g (5 oz) mozzarella
1 avocado, peeled, stoned and sliced
2 tbsp chopped fresh basil leaves

For the vinaigrette
1 tbsp balsamic vinegar
½ tsp caster sugar
1 tbsp soy sauce
4 tbsp light olive oil

1 Slice the tomatoes and mozzarella and arrange on a serving plate together with the sliced avocado.

2 Whisk together all the ingredients for the dressing and pour over the salad. Sprinkle over the basil and serve.

My favourite chicken and potato salad

MAKES 4 PORTIONS

I love tiny baby new potatoes – a lot of the goodness is in the skin.
The balsamic vinegar (and it's worth spending a little extra on a good one
to get the sweetness), chopped shallot and basil makes a delicious dressing.

PREP: 10 MINS
COOK: ABOUT 20 MINS
500 g (1 lb 2 oz) baby
  new potatoes
4 tbsp olive oil
1 red onion, finely sliced
1 garlic clove, crushed
1 tsp caster sugar
1 shallot, finely chopped
1½ tbsp balsamic vinegar
2 tbsp chopped fresh basil leaves
1 cooked chicken breast, sliced
salt and black pepper

1 Cook the potatoes in boiling salted water for
about 15 minutes until tender, then drain.

2 Heat 1 tablespoon of the olive oil in a saucepan.
Add the red onion and garlic and fry until soft.
Add the caster sugar and stir until lightly browned.
Tip into a bowl. Add the shallot, vinegar, basil
and remaining oil.

3 Slice the potatoes into thick slices. Add to
the salad with the chicken and season well.

Ratatouille omelette

SERVES 6

This concoction of sautéed Mediterranean vegetables mixed with eggs and topped with grated cheese in the style of a Spanish omelette is quite delicious and a meal in itself.

PREP: 10 MINS
COOK: ABOUT 35 MINS

3 tbsp olive oil
1 small onion, sliced
1 aubergine, sliced
1 large courgette, sliced
1 red pepper, deseeded
    and cut into strips
2 tomatoes, skinned,
    deseeded and chopped
6 medium eggs
25 g (1 oz) butter
5 tbsp double cream
75 g (3 oz) Gruyère cheese,
    grated
salt and black pepper

1 Heat the olive oil in a heavy-based frying pan and gently sauté the onion until soft. Chop the sliced aubergine and add with the courgette and red pepper, cover the pan and cook for about 20 minutes or until the vegetables are soft but not mushy. Add the tomatoes and cook for a further 5 minutes. Season to taste. Lightly whisk the eggs with 2 tablespoons of cold water, then mix in the cooked vegetables.

2 Preheat the grill medium-high. Heat the butter in a deep 25 cm (10 in) omelette or frying pan. When the butter is frothy, pour the egg mixture into the pan and cook until set. Remove from the heat, pour over the double cream and cover with the grated cheese. Cook under a preheated grill for a few minutes until golden. Leave the handle of the frying pan sticking out of the grill and cover with foil if necessary to prevent scorching.

Spaghetti with plum tomatoes and basil

MAKES 4 PORTIONS

A really good home-made tomato sauce is always popular. Choose the best-quality tomatoes you can afford to ensure they are packed with flavour.

PREP: 15 MINS
COOK: ABOUT 30 MINS

2 tbsp olive oil
1 onion, chopped
1 garlic clove, crushed
10 large ripe plum tomatoes,
    skinned, deseeded
    and chopped
1 tsp balsamic vinegar
1 tsp light soft brown sugar
a handful of basil leaves,
    torn into pieces
200 g (7 oz) spaghetti
salt and black pepper

1 Heat the olive oil in a saucepan and sauté the onion for 5–6 minutes until softened but not coloured. Add the garlic and sauté for 1 minute. Add the remaining ingredients, except the spaghetti, cover with a lid and cook over a medium heat for about 20 minutes.

2 Meanwhile, cook the pasta in a large saucepan of lightly salted water according to the packet instructions. Drain and serve topped with the sauce.

Mozzarella, pesto and tomato paninis

MAKES 2 PORTIONS (2 PANINIS)

Everyone loves a crunchy, hot panini and they are so simple to make at home. You can buy panini bread with the griddle marks on them so they look authentic even if you don't have a panini press.

PREP: 5 MINS
COOK: 4–6 MINS
2 paninis
a little butter, softened
2 tbsp pesto
250 g (8 oz) mozzarella, sliced
1 tomato, sliced
2 tbsp fresh basil leaves

1 Slice the paninis in half and lightly butter. Spread the pesto over 2 halves. Top with mozzarella, tomato and basil and sandwich together with the remaining halves.

2 Heat a frying pan until hot. Fry the paninis for 2–3 minutes on each side until crispy and the cheese is just melting.

Ham and cheese paninis

MAKES 2 PORTIONS (2 PANINIS)

Here's an alternative meaty filling – you could also use sliced turkey or chicken breast instead of the ham for a change.

PREP: 5 MINS
COOK: 4–6 MINS
2 paninis
a little butter
2 tbsp light mayonnaise
4 slices Gruyère cheese
4 slices ham

1 Slice the paninis in half. Lightly butter and spread 2 halves with the mayonnaise. Top with the cheese and ham and sandwich together with the remaining halves.

2 Heat a frying pan until hot. Fry the paninis for 2–3 minutes on each side until crispy and the cheese is just melting.

Club sandwich

Feel free to make up your own version here – for example using roast beef instead of pastrami and a little mustard.

PREP: 5 MINS
3 slices white bread
a little butter
1 tbsp light mayonnaise
25 g (1 oz) iceberg lettuce, shredded
1 slice Gruyère cheese
½ tomato sliced
2 slices pastrami
cocktail sticks
1 gherkin, sliced

1 Toast the bread in a toaster, then slice off the crusts. Butter each side and spread one slice with mayonnaise. Put some lettuce on top, then the cheese and tomato. Put a slice of bread on top, then more lettuce and pastrami. Top with the final slice and push down.

2 Slice into three fingers and use cocktail sticks to hold them in place. Top with a slice of gherkin.

Tuna melt

Try this nutritious, tasty, quick and easy snack.
If you wish you can use half-fat crème fraîche and
Cheddar cheese. This is also good for breakfast.

PREP: 5 MINS
COOK: 5 MINS

200 g (7 oz) can tuna in brine
2 tbsp tomato ketchup
2 tbsp crème fraîche
1 or 2 spring onions,
   finely sliced (optional)
2 English muffins
40 g (1½ oz) Cheddar
   cheese, grated

1 Preheat the grill to high. Drain the brine from the tuna and flake into small pieces. Mix together with the tomato ketchup, crème fraîche and spring onions (if using).

2 Split the muffins and toast them. Spread with the tuna mixture and sprinkle with the grated Cheddar. Place the muffins under the hot grill and grill until the cheese is golden and bubbling.

Prepare ahead

Annabel's granola

MAKES 6 PORTIONS

This delicious granola is very versatile and will keep in an airtight container for up to 4 weeks. You can have it for breakfast with milk. It's also very good on its own as a snack or layered with yoghurt, honey and fruit.

PREP: 10 MINS
COOK: 45 MINS

175 g (6 oz) rolled oats
70 g (2½ oz) coarsely chopped pecans
20 g (¾ oz) unsweetened desiccated coconut
¼ tsp salt
60 g (2½ oz) soft brown sugar
2 tbsp sunflower oil
4 tbsp maple syrup
50 g (2 oz) raisins

1 Preheat the oven to 150°C/300°F/Gas 2.

2 Put the oats, pecans, coconut, salt and sugar in a large bowl and mix together with a wooden spoon.

3 Whisk the oil and syrup together in a jug or small bowl. Pour over the oats and mix well.

4 Spread out on a lightly oiled baking sheet and bake in the centre of the oven for 40–45 minutes, stirring every 10 minutes. Transfer to a bowl, stir in the raisins and leave to cool.

Beef bourguignon

This delicious slow-cooked beef with fluffy dumplings makes a
perfect winter feast to keep you warm right down to your toes.

PREP: 15 MINS
COOK: 1¾–2¼ HOURS

2 tbsp olive oil
750 g (1 lb 10 oz) diced
   braising steak
200 g (7 oz) smoked
   bacon lardons
25g (1 oz) butter
2 large onions, sliced
2 garlic cloves, crushed
25 g (1 oz) plain flour
150 ml (5 fl oz) red wine
200 ml (7 fl oz) beef stock
1 tbsp redcurrant jelly
2 tsp chopped fresh thyme
200 g (7 oz) mushrooms,
   quartered

1 Heat 1 tablespoon of oil in a casserole. Brown the
beef in batches, then brown the bacon and set aside.

2 Melt the butter in the casserole. Add the onions and
sauté over the heat for 3–4 minutes. Add the garlic, then
the flour and stir until smooth, then blend in the wine
and stock. Add the jelly, thyme and browned beef and
bacon. Bring to the boil, cover and simmer gently on
the hob or place in a preheated oven (160°C/325°F/Gas 3)
for 1½–2 hours until tender.

3 Add the mushrooms 30 minutes before the end
of the cooking time.

Dumplings

These dumplings are so easy to prepare as an
extra accompaniment to this hearty stew.

PREP: 10 MINS
COOK: 20–30 MINS

85 g (3½ oz) self-raising flour
45 g (1½ oz) vegetable suet
1 tbsp chopped fresh parsley
salt and black pepper

1 Measure the flour, suet, parsley and 6 tablespoons
of water into a bowl. Season and mix together to make
a soft dough. Shape into 12 small balls.

2 Add the dumplings to the casserole at the same time
as the mushrooms, and continue to simmer on the hob
or in the oven, covered with a lid, for 20–30 minutes
until they have puffed up and are cooked through.

Lara's lasagne

This is one of my daughter Lara's favourite dishes and in winter it makes a good family meal. Lasagne freezes well and should be defrosted back to room temperature before baking until piping hot.

PREP: 20 MINS
COOK: 1 HOUR

1 tbsp olive oil
1 onion, chopped
1 garlic clove, crushed
½ red pepper, deseeded and chopped
450 g (1 lb) lean minced beef
½ tsp mixed freeze-dried herbs
400 g (14 oz) can chopped tomatoes, drained
295 g (10 oz) can condensed cream of tomato soup
9 sheets fresh or no pre-cook lasagne
25 g (1 oz) Parmesan cheese, grated
salt and black pepper

For the cheese sauce
50 g (2 oz) butter
40 g (1½ oz) plain flour
460 ml (16 fl oz) milk
a generous pinch of ground nutmeg
50 g (2 oz) Gruyère cheese, grated

1 Preheat the oven to 190°C/375°F/Gas 5.

2 Heat the olive oil in a large saucepan and sauté the onion, garlic and red pepper until softened. Add the beef and herbs and sauté until the beef has changed colour. Add the drained tomatoes and tomato soup and cook over a medium heat for 15–20 minutes. Season to taste.

3 Meanwhile, to prepare the cheese sauce, melt the butter, stir in the flour and cook for 1 minute. Gradually whisk in the milk, bring to the boil and whisk until thickened and smooth. Season with the nutmeg and a little salt and pepper. Remove from the heat and stir in the grated Gruyère until melted.

4 To assemble the lasagne, spoon a little of the meat sauce on to the base of an ovenproof dish, about 28 × 17 × 7 cm (11 × 6½ × 2¾ in). Cover with three sheets of lasagne. Divide the remaining meat sauce in half and cover the lasagne with half of it. Spoon over a little of the cheese sauce.

5 Cover with three more sheets of lasagne and cover with the remaining meat sauce. Again spoon over a little of the cheese sauce but make sure that enough remains to completely cover the top layer of lasagne. Arrange the remaining sheets of lasagne on top and then spread over the remaining cheese sauce so that the lasagne is completely covered. Sprinkle over the Parmesan and bake for 25–30 minutes.

Lasagne with spinach, cheese and tomato

MAKES 4 PORTIONS

This is my favourite vegetarian lasagne. If you can find sheets of
fresh lasagne, I think they taste better than dried. If using the dried lasagne,
you may need to cook this for 5 minutes longer and make sure that the
lasagne is completely covered with sauce or it will dry out.

PREP: 20 MINS
COOK: 35 MINS

225 g (8 oz) frozen or 450 g (1 lb)
  fresh spinach
15 g (½ oz) butter
175 g (6 oz) cottage cheese
1 medium egg, lightly beaten
2 tbsp double cream
25 g (1 oz) Parmesan cheese,
  grated
6 sheets lasagne (fresh or dried)
125 g (4½ oz) mozzarella cheese,
  grated
15 g/½ oz Gruyère cheese, grated
salt and black pepper

For the tomato sauce
1 tbsp olive oil
1 onion, chopped
1 garlic clove, crushed
2 tbsp tomato purée
2 × 400 g (14 oz) cans chopped
  tomatoes
1 tbsp chopped fresh parsley
1 tbsp chopped fresh basil leaves
1 tsp dried oregano
½ tsp caster sugar

1 Preheat the oven to 180°C/350°F/Gas 4.

2 To make the tomato sauce, heat the olive oil in a
saucepan and sauté the onion and garlic until softened.
Add the tomato purée and sauté for 1 minute. Drain and
discard the juice from the cans of tomatoes and add the
tomatoes to the sautéed onions. Add all the remaining
ingredients and simmer, uncovered, for 10 minutes.
Season to taste.

3 Meanwhile, to prepare the spinach and cheese layer,
wilt the spinach, drain thoroughly and then sauté in the
butter for a couple of minutes. In a food processor, blend
together the spinach, cottage cheese, egg, double cream
and Parmesan. Season with a little black pepper.

4 To assemble the lasagne, spread a thin layer of the
tomato sauce over the base of a fairly deep ovenproof
dish measuring about 23 × 15 cm (9 × 6 in). Lay two
sheets of lasagne on top. Cover with half the spinach
mixture, one-third of the mozzarella and one-third
of the tomato sauce. Again, lay two sheets of lasagne
on top, spoon the remaining spinach mixture on top
and then cover with half the remaining mozzarella
and half the remaining tomato sauce.

5 Lay the remaining two sheets of lasagne on top,
cover with the remaining tomato sauce and mozzarella
and then sprinkle the Gruyère over the top. Bake for
about 25 minutes.

Easy beef casserole

MAKES 4 PORTIONS

Cooking this casserole slowly makes the beef very tender and all the flavours mingle together. It will happily sit in the fridge for 24 hours before adding the crème fraîche, reheating then serving with rice or potatoes.

PREP: 10 MINS
COOK: I HOUR 45 MINS

1 tbsp vegetable oil
500 g (1 lb 2 oz) beef
    (braising or stewing), diced
1 large onion, sliced
1 red pepper, deseeded and diced
2 garlic cloves, crushed
1 tbsp paprika
1½ tbsp tomato purée
2 tsp beef stock
1½ tsp balsamic vinegar
½ tsp dark soft brown sugar
½ tsp Worcestershire sauce
6 tbsp full-fat crème fraîche

1 Preheat the oven to 180°C/350°F/Gas 4.

2 Heat the oil in a frying pan. Brown the beef on all sides until golden, then transfer to a plate. Add the onion to the pan with the red pepper and fry for 3–4 minutes. Add the garlic, paprika and tomato purée and fry for about 2 minutes. Return the beef to the pan and coat in the onion mixture, then add 350 ml (12 fl oz) water and the beef stock and bring to the boil. Cover with a lid and bake in the oven for 1 hour.

3 Remove from the oven and add the remaining ingredients. Bring back to the boil, cover and put back into the oven for another 30–40 minutes or until the beef is tender. Serve with rice or mash.

Tarragon chicken casserole

MAKES 4 PORTIONS

Tarragon and chicken are the perfect pairing in this creamy one-pot dinner.
I also like to make this with a mixture of chicken thighs and part-boned chicken
breasts because some of my family prefer white meat to brown. You can make
this 24 hours in advance, cool and keep in the fridge until you are ready
to reheat and serve. It's perfect with a green salad and mashed potato.

PREP: 15 MINS
COOK: 50 MINS
8 chicken thighs, skinned
2 tbsp olive oil
2 onions, chopped
1 garlic clove, crushed
15g butter
25 g (1 oz) plain flour
150 ml (5 fl oz) white wine
200 ml (7 fl oz) chicken stock
150 g (5 oz) mushrooms,
    quartered
3 tbsp double cream
1½ tbsp chopped fresh tarragon
salt and black pepper

1 Preheat the oven to 160°C/325°F/Gas 3.

2 Season the thighs, then heat 1 tablespoon of the
oil in a casserole. Brown the thighs and set aside.

3 Heat the remaining oil in the pan. Add the onions
and garlic and fry for 3 minutes. Add the butter then
sprinkle in the flour and stir until smooth. Add the
wine and stock, stirring until blended. Return the
chicken to the pan and bring to the boil, cover and
simmer in the oven for 45 minutes. Add the mushrooms
20 minutes before the end of the cooking time. Add
the cream and stir through. Season to taste and
sprinkle with tarragon before serving.

Moroccan lamb tagine

MAKES 4–6 PORTIONS

This tagine actually tastes better if you make it a day ahead because
the flavours of the lamb, spices and apricots will meld over time.

PREP: 10 MINS
COOK: 1 HOUR 40 MINS

2 tbsp vegetable oil
1 kg (2¼ lb) lamb neck
    fillet, diced
2 onions, sliced
1 garlic clove, crushed
1 tbsp grated fresh ginger
2 tsp ground cinnamon
1 tbsp ground cumin
1 tbsp ground coriander
400 g (14 oz) can of chopped
    tomatoes
1½ tbsp tomato purée
6 dried apricots, chopped
1½ tbsp honey
juice of ½ lemon
salt and black pepper

1 Preheat the oven to 160°C/325°F/Gas 3.

2 Heat 1 tablespoon of the oil in a casserole. Brown
the lamb in batches and set aside.

3 Heat the remaining oil in the pan, add the onions,
garlic and ginger and fry for 3–4 minutes. Add the
spices, tomatoes, purée, apricots, honey and lemon
juice. Bring to the boil, cover and simmer on the
hob or in the oven for 1½ hours until tender. Season
to taste before serving. Serve with couscous and
sprinkled with a handful of pinenuts and chopped
flat-leaf parsley, if you like.

Spiced butternut squash soup

MAKES 4 PORTIONS

Come in from the cold to this delicious, warming
bowl of soup that's flavoured with fresh ginger and chilli –
it's oh so simple to prepare. You can freeze this soup.

PREP: 10 MINS
COOK: 25 MINS

15 g (½ oz) butter
1 onion, chopped
2 celery sticks, diced
150 g (5 oz) carrots, diced
200 g (7 oz) butternut
    squash, chopped
½ red chilli, deseeded and diced
1 tsp grated fresh ginger
450 ml (¾ pint) chicken or
    vegetable stock
salt and black pepper

1 Melt the butter in a saucepan, then add the vegetables, chilli and ginger. Sauté the veg for 8–10 minutes, until almost softened. Add the stock and bring to the boil.

2 Simmer, covered, for 15 minutes or until the vegetables are tender. Blend in a food processor or blender until smooth. Season to taste before serving.

Mediterranean tomato soup

MAKES 6 PORTIONS

This tomato soup has a wonderful flavour. It's a great recipe to encourage children to eat different kinds of vegetables. This soup can also be frozen.

PREP: 10 MINS
COOK: 40-45 MINS
2 tbsp olive oil
25 g (1 oz) butter
2 onions, diced
2 carrots, diced
2 celery sticks, diced
1 garlic clove, crushed
1½ tbsp roughly chopped fresh basil leaves
1½ tbsp roughly chopped fresh tarragon
1 bay leaf
500 g (1 lb 2 oz) ripe plum tomatoes, skinned, quartered and deseeded
400 g (14 oz) can chopped tomatoes
1 tbsp tomato purée
600 ml (1 pint) chicken stock
salt and black pepper

1 Heat the olive oil and butter in a large saucepan and sauté the onions, carrots and celery for 2–3 minutes. Add the garlic, herbs and bay leaf and cook for 7–8 minutes. Add the fresh and canned tomatoes and cook over a low heat for about 15 minutes.

2 Stir in the tomato purée and gradually add the stock. Cook over a medium heat for 15 minutes. Remove the bay leaf and blend in a food processor or blender. Season to taste before serving.

Onion soup

MAKES 8 PORTIONS

This warming soup has a delicious flavour as I allow the onions to caramelise to bring out their sweetness. You can also mix ordinary onions with red onions. If you wish, make the soup up to step 3 the day before and keep in the fridge ready to reheat and serve with it's cheesy topping. It's great comfort food on a cold winter's night.

PREP: 15 MINS
COOK: 1 HOUR 20 MINS
2 tbsp olive oil
50 g (2 oz) butter
550 g (1¼ lb) onions, thinly sliced
1 garlic clove, crushed
½ tsp granulated sugar
1.2 litres (2 pints) beef stock
1 large potato, peeled and cubed
150 ml (¼ pint) dry white wine
½ French baguette
75 g (3 oz) Gruyère cheese, grated
salt and black pepper

1 Melt the olive oil and butter in a large casserole. Add the onions, garlic and sugar and cook over a medium heat, stirring until the onions have browned. Reduce the heat to the lowest setting, cover the onions with a sheet of non-stick baking paper and leave the onions to cook slowly for about 30 minutes.

2 Meanwhile, put half the stock into a saucepan, add the cubed potato and cook for 10–12 minutes or until the potato is soft. Blend the potato with some of the stock in a food processor or blender. This will help thicken the soup.

3 Remove the non-stick baking paper and pour the thickened stock, the remaining beef stock and the wine over the caramelised onions. Season, then stir with a wooden spoon, scraping the base of the pan to get the full flavour of the caramelised onions. Simmer gently, uncovered, for 30 minutes.

4 To make the cheesy French bread slices to float on top of the soup, first preheat the grill to high. Cut the loaf diagonally into 12 mm (½ in) slices and toast lightly on both sides. Pour the soup into individual ovenproof bowls and top each one with a slice of bread. Sprinkle the bread liberally with the grated Gruyère. Place the bowls under the hot grill until the cheese is melted and bubbling. Serve immediately.

Multi-layered cottage pie

This is a rather luxurious version of an old-fashioned favourite comfort food.
You can either make one large cottage pie or several individual portions in ramekin
dishes so that you can freeze some portions for use later. It looks especially good
in a clear Pyrex dish so you can see the colourful layers. You can also substitute
lamb mince for minced beef to turn this into a Shepherd's Pie, if preferred.

PREP: 30 MINS
COOK: 45 MINS

450 g (1 lb) carrots, chopped
a generous knob of butter
2½ tbsp vegetable oil
450 g (1 lb) minced beef
1 large onion, finely chopped
100 g (4 oz) leek, finely chopped
100 g (4 oz) red pepper, deseeded
    and finely chopped
1 garlic clove, crushed
150 g (5 oz) button
    mushrooms, sliced
1 tbsp tomato purée
400 g (14 oz) can chopped
    tomatoes, drained
2 tsp Worcestershire sauce
½ tsp dried mixed herbs
1 beef stock cube dissolved in
    300 ml (½ pint) boiling water
salt and black pepper

For the topping
675 g (1 lb 4 oz) potatoes,
    peeled and cut into chunks
50 g (2 oz) unsalted butter
6 tbsp milk
200 g (7 oz) frozen peas, cooked
1 medium egg, beaten
salt and white pepper

1 Cook the carrots in a saucepan of lightly salted
boiling water for 20 minutes or until tender, then
mash with the butter until smooth.

2 Heat ½ tablespoon of the oil in a large non-stick
frying pan and sauté the beef mince for 7–8 minutes
or until all the liquid has evaporated. Remove the
beef from the pan and set aside.

3 Heat the remaining oil in a large casserole and
sauté the onion and leek for 5 minutes. Add the red
pepper and sauté for 3 minutes, then add the garlic
and sauté for 30 seconds. Add the mushrooms and
sauté for 2 minutes. Add the tomato purée, tomatoes,
Worcestershire sauce, herbs and beef stock, and
simmer for about 30 minutes. Season to taste.

4 Meanwhile make the topping: boil the potatoes for
15–20 minutes, then drain. Return the cooked potatoes
to the empty saucepan and mash together with the
butter, milk, salt and white pepper until smooth.

5 Preheat the oven to 180°C/350°F/Gas 4. Place the
mashed carrots in the base of a glass ovenproof
dish or use mini dishes to make individual portions.
Arrange the meat on top, then cover with a layer of
cooked peas and top with a layer of potato. Brush
the potato with the beaten egg and cook in the oven
for 15–20 minutes. Brown the top under the grill,
if neccesary, before serving.

Mini fish pies

MAKES 4–6 PORTIONS

I love to make fish pie in individual portions with fresh dill.
The fish goes in raw, along with the frozen peas, so that they are
not overcooked. Try these pies with a carrot and potato mash
too; simply swap half the potato quantity for carrots.

PREP: 20 MINS
COOK: ABOUT 50 MINS

700 g (1½ lb) potatoes
(Maris Piper and King
Edward work well)
30 g (1¼ oz) butter
6 tbsp milk
300 g (10 oz) salmon, skin
removed and cut into
2 cm (¾ in) chunks
300 g (10 oz) cod, skin removed
and cut into 2 cm (¾ in) chunks
75 g (3 oz) frozen peas
1 medium egg, lightly beaten
salt and black pepper

For the sauce
45 g (1½ oz) butter
1 large banana shallot, diced
2 tbsp white wine vinegar
45 g (1½ oz) plain flour
450 ml (15 fl oz) fish stock
40 g (1½ oz) Parmesan cheese,
freshly grated
6 tbsp double cream
1 tbsp chopped fresh dill

1 Preheat the oven to 200°C/400°F/Gas 6.

2 Boil the potatoes in salted water. Drain and mash
with the butter and milk and season to taste.

3 To make the sauce, melt the butter and sauté the
shallot for 5–6 minutes until soft. Add the white wine
vinegar and boil for 2–3 minutes until the liquid has
evaporated. Stir in the flour to make a roux. Gradually
stir in the fish stock and then cook over a medium heat,
stirring continuously. Bring to the boil and then cook,
stirring until thickened. Add the Parmesan and mix
to melt then remove from the heat and stir in the
cream and the chopped dill. Season well.

4 Divide the fish and peas between six mini ramekins
(10 × 5 cm/4 × 2 in) pour over the sauce and cover with
the mashed potato. Alternatively, you can make one
large fish pie in an ovenproof dish. Brush the potato
topping with a little egg. Bake for 20–25 minutes.
Finish off under a preheated grill to brown the top,
if necessary.

Tuna tagliatelle bake

MAKES 6 PORTIONS

This is a tasty and nutritious pasta dish that is quick and easy to make for
the whole family using store cupboard ingredients, including a can of tomato soup.
Make this recipe a day in advance then keep it chilled in the fridge ready to bake.

PREP: 15 MINS
COOK: ABOUT 35 MINS

225 g (8 oz) green and
    white tagliatelle
25 g (1 oz) butter
1 small onion, finely chopped
1 heaped tbsp cornflour
405 g (14 oz) can cream
    of tomato soup
2 tbsp chopped fresh parsley
½ tsp dried mixed herbs
400 g (14 oz) can tuna in oil,
    well drained

For the cheese sauce
25 g (1 oz) butter
20 g (¾ oz) flour
375 ml (12 fl oz) milk
a pinch of dried mustard powder
100 g (4 oz) Cheddar cheese,
    grated
1 tbsp snipped fresh chives
50 g (2 oz) sweetcorn, cooked
salt and black pepper

For the topping
25 g (1 oz) brown breadcrumbs
25 g (1 oz) Cheddar cheese, grated
1 tbsp freshly grated
    Parmesan cheese

1 Preheat the oven to 180°C/350°F/Gas 4.

2 Cook the tagliatelle in a large saucepan of lightly salted
boiling water according to the packet instructions until
just tender, then drain.

3 Meanwhile, melt the butter in another saucepan
and sauté the onion until softened. Mix the cornflour
with 2 tablespoons of cold water until dissolved. Mix
the cornflour mixture, tomato soup, parsley and herbs
with the sautéed onion and cook over a medium heat
for about 5 minutes or until the sauce has thickened.
Stir the tuna into the sauce and mix with the
cooked tagliatelle.

4 To make the cheese sauce, put the butter, flour and
milk into a saucepan and cook over a medium heat.
Using a balloon whisk, keep whisking the mixture until
it boils and thickens to form a smooth sauce. Add the
mustard powder and simmer for 2–3 minutes. Remove
from the heat and stir in 75 g (3 oz) of the cheese until
melted. Stir in the chives and cooked sweetcorn and
season to taste.

5 Arrange the tuna and pasta mixture in a 25 × 20 cm
(10 × 8 in) ovenproof dish and pour over the cheese
sauce. Mix together the breadcrumbs and grated cheeses
for the topping and scatter these over the top. Bake for
20 minutes, then brown under a preheated grill for
a few minutes before serving.

Meatballs in tomato and basil sauce

MAKES 4 PORTIONS

A hearty, simple-to-make recipe. Instead of using breadcrumbs, I use pieces of bread soaked in milk, which keeps the meatballs really moist.

PREP: 15 MINS
COOK: 30 MINS

75 g (3 oz) white bread, torn into pieces
5 tbsp milk
250 g (9 oz) lean minced beef
1 medium egg yolk
2 tsp dried oregano
50 g (2 oz) Parmesan cheese, grated
2 tbsp olive oil
1 onion, chopped
1 garlic clove, crushed
400 g (14 oz) can chopped tomatoes
150 ml (¼ pint) beef stock
1 tbsp tomato purée
3 tbsp chopped fresh basil leaves
salt and black pepper

1 Put the pieces of bread into a bowl. Add the milk and leave to soak for 5 minutes, then mash with a fork. Add the beef, egg yolk, dried oregano and Parmesan and season. Shape into 20 balls.

2 Heat 1 tablespoon of the olive oil and fry the meatballs for about 4 minutes or until browned then set aside.

3 Heat the remaining olive oil in a saucepan. Add the onion and garlic and fry for 5 minutes. Add the tomatoes, stock and purée and bring to the boil. Add the meatballs, cover and simmer for 20 minutes. Stir in the basil before serving.

Veggie sausages

MAKES 8 SAUSAGES

A very tasty way to get one or two of your five a day. You can make up batches of these and freeze them in advance. Cook them in the oven from frozen at 180°C/350°F/Gas 4 for 20 minutes. Or defrost and fry as below.

PREP: 15 MINS
COOK: 20 MINS
150 g (5 oz) white potato, unpeeled
150 g (5 oz) sweet potato, unpeeled
1 tbsp olive oil
2 leeks, chopped
2 carrots, grated
6 mushrooms, grated
1 garlic clove, crushed
40 g (1½ oz) breadcrumbs
40 g (1½ oz) Parmesan cheese, grated
a little plain flour, for coating
sunflower oil, for frying
salt and black pepper

1 Prick the potatoes with a fork. Put into the microwave and cook for 10 minutes until soft. Scoop out the potato and mash in a bowl.

2 Heat the olive oil in a frying pan. Add the leeks, carrots, mushrooms and garlic and fry for 5 minutes until soft. Add to a bowl with the breadcrumbs and Parmesan cheese. Season and shape into 8 sausages.

3 Coat the sausages in flour, then fry in a little sunflower oil for about 4 minutes or until golden on all sides.

Veggie burgers

These veg-packed burgers are delicious eaten either hot
or cold. Make them the day before, if you like, and leave in
the fridge overnight ready to cook the following day.

PREP: 20 MINS
COOK: 10 MINS

2 carrots, grated
1 courgette, grated
1 onion, chopped
50 g (2 oz) chestnut or button
   mushrooms, chopped
75 g (3 oz) cashew nuts,
   roughly chopped
1 tbsp chopped fresh oregano
   or ½ tsp dried oregano
1 tbsp chopped fresh parsley
a pinch of cayenne pepper
   (optional)
250 g (9 oz) fresh brown
   breadcrumbs
1 tbsp tomato sauce
½ tbsp soy sauce
½ medium egg yolk
vegetable oil, for frying
salt and black pepper

1 Using your hands, squeeze out some of the excess
moisture from the grated carrots and courgette. In
a large bowl, mix together all the vegetables, cashew
nuts, herbs, cayenne pepper, if using, and 150 g (5 oz)
of the breadcrumbs.

2 Beat together the tomato sauce, soy sauce and
the half egg yolk. Stir this into the vegetable mixture
and season. Using your hands, form the mixture into
8 burgers and coat with the remaining breadcrumbs.
At this stage you can set the burgers aside in the
fridge to firm up, but it is not essential.

3 Heat the oil and sauté the burgers in batches
for 2 minutes on each side or until they are golden.
Drain on kitchen paper, before serving.

Yummy burgers

MAKES 8 BURGERS

Making your own 'healthy junk food' is one way to encourage everyone in your family to eat better quality food. It's best to freeze burgers uncooked on a tray lined with clingfilm. Then, when frozen, wrap them individually in clingfilm and pop them in a plastic freezer box. You can then remove and use as many as you like.

PREP: 15 MINS
COOK: 12 MINS

1 tbsp sunflower oil
1 large red onion, finely chopped
1 garlic clove, crushed
2 tsp fresh thyme leaves
2 tbsp chopped fresh parsley
400 g (14 oz) lean minced beef
1 eating apple, peeled, cored and
    grated (Pink Lady, Granny
    Smith and Gala all work well)
1 medium egg yolk
2 tbsp tomato chutney
1 chicken stock cube, crumbled
2 slices white bread,
    made into breadcrumbs
salt and black pepper

1 Heat the oil in a frying pan and sauté the onion over a low heat for about 6 minutes until softened. Add the garlic, thyme and parsley and continue to cook for 1 minute. Leave the mixture to cool down.

2 Mix the minced beef with the grated apple, egg yolk, tomato chutney, crumbled chicken stock cube and fresh breadcrumbs and season to taste.

3 Preheat the grill to medium-high. Shape the mixture into 8 burgers and place on a non-stick baking tray. Grill the burgers for 5 minutes on each side or until cooked. Serve in buns with extra chutney and a salad garnish.

Weekend get-togethers

Perfect pancakes

MAKES 12 PANCAKES

Pancakes for breakfast are a real treat and you can make delicious, really thin pancakes with this foolproof batter. Sprinkle them with lemon juice and dust with icing sugar or serve with maple or golden syrup and perhaps some fresh fruit. These pancakes can be made in advance, refrigerated and then reheated just before serving. Pancakes also freeze very well. Interleave with non-stick baking paper, then wrap in foil and freeze for up to a month. Thaw at room temperature for several hours.

PREP: 10 MINS
COOK: 25 MINS
100 g (4 oz) plain flour
a generous pinch of salt
2 medium eggs
300 ml (10 fl oz) milk
50 g (2 oz) butter, melted

1 Sift the flour with a big pinch of salt into a mixing bowl, make a well in the centre and add the eggs. Use a balloon whisk to incorporate the eggs into the flour. Gradually whisk in the milk. Stir the mixture until smooth but do not overmix.

2 Use a heavy-based 15–18 cm (6–7 in) frying pan and brush with the melted butter (either use a pastry brush or some crumpled kitchen paper to coat the base of the pan). When hot, pour in about 2 tablespoons of the batter. Quickly tilt the pan from side to side until you get a thin layer of batter covering the base of the frying pan.

3 Cook the pancake for about 1 minute, then flip it over (you can use a spatula for this) and cook until the underside is lightly flecked with gold. Keep warm while you continue with the rest of the batter, brushing the pan with melted butter when necessary.

Thai-style chicken soup

MAKES 4 PORTIONS

There's no need to order a Friday night takeaway as this healthy soup is quick, easy and satisfying. Add more chilli if you want to spice it up a little.

PREP: 20 MINS
COOK: 12 MINS

1 tbsp light olive oil
150 g (5 oz) chopped onion
1 garlic clove, crushed
½ red chilli, deseeded and finely
　chopped (about 1 tbsp)
1 skinless chicken breast fillet,
　cut into thin strips
100 g (4 oz) broccoli, cut into
　florets
600 ml (1 pint) chicken stock
300 ml (½ pint) coconut milk
150 g (5 oz) cooked rice
　(40 g/1½ oz uncooked weight)
salt and black pepper

1 Heat the olive oil in a saucepan and sauté the onion, garlic and chilli for 2 minutes. Add the strips of chicken and sauté for 2 more minutes.

2 Add the broccoli and chicken stock to the pan, bring to the boil and simmer for 4 minutes. Stir in the coconut milk and simmer for 2 minutes. Season to taste and stir in the cooked rice.

Summer risotto

MAKES 4 PORTIONS

I like to make my risotto in a large frying pan. You will need to add the liquid to the rice little by little, waiting to add more until all the liquid has been absorbed and stirring frequently. It usually takes about 30 minutes to prepare, depending on your pan and your hob.

PREP: 10 MINS
COOK: 20-25 MINS
900 ml (1½ pints) vegetable or chicken stock
1 tbsp olive oil
40 g (½ oz) butter
4 large shallots or 1 onion, finely chopped
1 garlic clove, crushed
50 g (2 oz) red pepper, deseeded and chopped
200 g (7 oz) risotto rice
75 g (3 oz) courgette, diced
2 tomatoes, skinned, deseeded and chopped (about 225 g/8 oz)
4 tbsp white wine
40 g (½ oz) Parmesan cheese, grated
salt and black pepper

1 Bring the stock to the boil in a saucepan and leave to simmer. Heat the olive oil and butter in a large frying pan and sauté the shallots and garlic for 1 minute. Add the red pepper and cook for 5 minutes, stirring occasionally until softened.

2 Add the rice and make sure that it is well coated. Stir for 1 minute. Add 1–2 ladlefuls of hot stock at a time, stirring until absorbed. Add a ladleful of hot stock, stirring until absorbed.

3 After 10 minutes, add the diced courgette and tomato. After about 8 minutes add the white wine.

4 When all the stock has been added and the rice is cooked (this will take about 20 minutes), stir in the Parmesan until melted and season to taste.

Squash, pea and sage risotto

MAKES 4 PORTIONS

Butternut squash with fresh Parmesan and sage is one of my favourite flavour combinations for a risotto.

PREP: 10 MINS
COOK: 25 MINS

1 tbsp olive oil
2 leeks, chopped
1 garlic clove, crushed
250 g (9 oz) risotto rice
150 g (5 oz) butternut squash, diced
1 litre (1¾ pints) hot chicken stock
50g peas
1 tsp chopped fresh sage
50 g (2 oz) Parmesan cheese, grated
1 tsp lemon juice
2 tbsp double cream
salt and black pepper

1 Heat the olive oil in a saucepan. Add the leeks and fry for 3 minutes. Add the garlic, rice and squash and stir to make sure the rice is well coated.

2 Add a ladleful of hot stock at a time, stirring until absorbed.

3 When all the stock has been added and the rice is cooked (this will take about 20 minutes) add the peas and sage and stir for the last 5 minutes. Stir in the Parmesan, lemon juice and cream and season to taste.

Chicken fajitas

MAKES 8 FAJITAS

These are a great favourite of mine and I have made them much less hot and spicy so that children will enjoy eating them. When they were little, my children loved to assemble these and roll them up themselves. Everything can be prepared in advance. If you want to save time then you can use a ready-made salsa.

PREP: 15 MINS
COOK: 25 MINS

2 small skinless chicken breasts, cut into strips
⅛ tsp paprika
⅛ tsp mild chilli powder
⅛ tsp ground cumin
¼ tsp dried oregano
1½ tbsp olive oil
1 garlic clove, crushed
1 onion, thinly sliced
½ small red pepper, deseeded and thinly sliced
8 small flour tortillas
75 g (3 oz) iceberg lettuce, shredded
75 g (3 oz) Cheddar cheese, grated
4 tbsp soured cream
salt and black pepper

For the tomato salsa
½ tbsp olive oil
¼ green chilli, deseeded and finely sliced
½ onion, chopped
¼ small red pepper, deseeded and diced
1 small garlic clove, crushed
½ tsp red wine vinegar
200 g (7 oz) can chopped tomatoes
½ tbsp chopped fresh parsley

1 Toss the chicken strips in the paprika, chilli powder, cumin and oregano. Heat 1 teaspoon of the olive oil in a pan and sauté the chicken, stirring occasionally, for 3–4 minutes. Remove the chicken with a slotted spoon. Add the remaining oil and sauté the garlic, onion and red pepper for 5 minutes. Return the chicken to the pan, season to taste and heat through.

2 Meanwhile make the tomato salsa. Heat the olive oil and fry the chilli, onion, pepper and garlic for about 5 minutes. Add the vinegar and cook for about 20 seconds. Add the chopped tomatoes and parsley, season to taste and simmer, uncovered, for about 15 minutes.

3 To assemble, heat the tortillas in the microwave according to the packet instructions. Place some of the chicken mixture along the centre of each tortilla, top with some tomato salsa, shredded lettuce, grated cheese and a little soured cream and roll up.

Roast leg of lamb

MAKES 6 PORTIONS

The lamb is also good eaten cold the next day. Ask your butcher to butterfly
a leg of lamb for you – you will end up with a boned, flattened cut of lamb
that is easy to carve and takes much less time to cook. This can be served with
couscous mixed with some diced roasted vegetables like aubergine, courgette,
onion and sweet pepper. It is also absolutely delicious cooked on a barbecue;
cook over indirect heat for about 1 hour or until cooked through.

PREP: 10 MINS,
PLUS MARINATING
AND RESTING TIME
COOK: 40-60 MINS

1 leg of lamb, boned
    and butterflied

For the marinade
150 ml (¼ pint) oil
2 tbsp walnut oil
150 ml (¼ pint) red wine
2 tsp chopped fresh oregano
4 tbsp lemon juice
2–3 garlic cloves, crushed
2 tbsp chopped fresh parsley
1 tsp sea salt
¼ tsp black pepper

1 Mix all the ingredients for the marinade together.
Trim away as much excess fat from the lamb as you
can. Pierce the lamb all over with the sharp point of a
knife and place in a large polythene bag together with
the marinade. Tie up the bag and leave in the fridge for
12–24 hours, turning frequently until ready to cook.

2 Preheat the oven to 220°C/425°F/Gas 7. Remove the
lamb from the marinade and place on a rack over a
roasting tin. Roast in the oven for between 40 minutes
and 1 hour depending on its weight and how you like
it cooked. Take the lamb out of the oven and let it rest
under foil for 15–20 minutes before carving across
the grain into slices.

Roasted chicken breasts with sweet peppers

MAKES 4 PORTIONS

This is one of my favourite ways to cook chicken because it manages to keep the meat so lovely and moist, and it is all roasted in one tin to save on washing up!

PREP: 15 MINS
COOK: 50-60 MINS

500 g (1 lb 2 oz) baby new potatoes
1 red pepper, deseeded and sliced into large pieces
1 yellow pepper, deseeded and sliced into large pieces
1 red onion, sliced into wedges
3 tbsp olive oil
2 tbsp chopped fresh thyme
1 tbsp honey
2 garlic cloves, crushed
4 part-boned chicken breasts, skin on
175 ml (6 fl oz) white wine
50 ml (2 fl oz) chicken stock
salt and black pepper

1 Preheat the oven to 220°C/425°F/ Gas 7.

2 Slice the potatoes in half or into quarters if they are quite large. Put the potatoes in a roasting tin along with the peppers and onion. Drizzle over 2 tablespoons of the olive oil and half the thyme. Season. Roast for 30 minutes.

3 Mix the remaining oil, honey and thyme with the garlic in a small bowl. Rub all over the chicken breasts and under the skin to make sure they are well coated.

4 Pour the wine and chicken stock over the vegetables then place the chicken pieces on top. Roast for a further 25–30 minutes until the chicken is golden and cooked through and the vegetables are tender.

Roast chicken with squash and red onion

MAKES 4–6 PORTIONS

Roast chicken is always a crowd pleaser. Adding potatoes, butternut squash and red onion to the roasting tin infuses them with lovely chicken flavour and goes perfectly with my white-wine gravy.

PREP: 20 MINS
COOK: 1¼–1¾ HOURS

50 g (2 oz) butter, softened
1 tbsp chopped fresh tarragon
1 tbsp chopped fresh chives
1.5 kg (3¼ lb) roasting chicken
1 small butternut squash
3 large potatoes, peeled
2 red onions, sliced into wedges
3 tbsp olive oil
juice of 1 lemon
salt and black pepper

For the gravy
20 g (¾ oz) butter
20 g (¾ oz) plain flour
100 ml (3½ fl oz) white wine
250 ml (8 fl oz) chicken stock
a few drops Worcestershire sauce
sprinkle of caster sugar

1 Preheat the oven to 220°C/425°F/Gas 7.

2 Put the butter, herbs and seasoning in a small bowl and mash together. Loosen the skin over the breast of the chicken and spread the butter underneath using your hands. Season and place in the middle of a roasting tray.

3 Peel and cut the squash into 3 cm (1¼ in) pieces. Cut the potatoes into 3 cm (1¼ in) pieces. Put the vegetables into a bowl. Season and toss in the olive oil. Arrange around the chicken in the roasting tray and squeeze over the lemon. Roast for 1–1½ hours until golden and cooked through. Turn the vegetables halfway through the cooking time.

4 To make the gravy, melt the butter in a saucepan. Add the flour and whisk together. Blend in the wine and stock and any cooking juices from the chicken. Stir until slightly thickened. Add the Worcestershire sauce and the sugar to taste. Serve the chicken and vegetables with the gravy.

Courgette gratin

MAKES 6 PORTIONS

This has a light soufflé-type consistency. It makes a delicious light
lunch with a crisp, green salad, can be served as a tasty accompaniment
to a meal and it looks elegant enough for a dinner party.

PREP: 10 MINS
COOK: 40–45 MINS
3 tbsp vegetable oil
500 g (1 lb 2 oz) courgettes,
    topped and tailed and
    thinly sliced
2 tbsp chopped fresh parsley
4 medium eggs
125 ml (4 fl oz) crème fraîche
150 g (5 oz) Gruyère cheese,
    grated
salt and black pepper

1 Preheat the oven to 180°C/350°F/Gas 4.

2 Heat the oil in a frying pan and season the courgettes
with some salt and pepper. Sauté these together with
the parsley over a low heat for about 20 minutes or until
softened. Using a fork, beat the eggs, then beat in the
crème fraîche, Gruyère and a little seasoning. Stir in the
courgettes then spoon the mixture into an ovenproof
dish measuring about 25 × 20 cm (10 × 8 in). Bake in
the oven for 20–25 minutes until golden on top.

Chicken yakitori with noodles

MAKES 4 PORTIONS

Traditionally this is made with chicken thigh, which is more moist than chicken breast and contains twice as much iron and zinc as white meat. The sticky sweetness of the marinade gives a delicious flavour to the meat.

**PREP: 15 MINS, PLUS MARINATING TIME
COOK: 20-25 MINS**

3 tbsp mirin
3 tbsp soy sauce
3 tbsp honey
2 tsp rice wine vinegar
1 tsp grated fresh ginger
1 garlic clove, crushed
4 boneless chicken thighs, cut into large chunks
3 tbsp vegetable oil
125 g (4½ oz) medium noodles
1 large courgette, sliced into batons
1 large carrot, sliced into batons
2 spring onions, thinly sliced
1 red onion, sliced
75 g (3 oz) chestnut mushrooms, sliced
5 tbsp chicken stock
4 tsp soy sauce
4 tsp sweet chilli sauce
salt and black pepper

1 Preheat the oven to 220°C/425°F/Gas 7. If you are using wooden skewers, soak them in water for 30 minutes to prevent scorching.

2 Bring the mirin, soy sauce, honey, vinegar, ginger and garlic to the boil in a small saucepan, then boil to reduce by a third, stirring. Leave to cool.

3 Mix the cold marinade with the chicken and leave to marinate for 30 minutes. Season and thread onto 4 skewers. Heat the oil in a frying pan. Brown the skewers for 1–2 minutes on both sides until golden, then place onto a baking sheet and continue to cook in the oven for 12–15 minutes until cooked through.

4 Meanwhile, cook the noodles. Heat the remaining oil in a frying pan or wok. Fry all the vegetables for about 3–4 minutes, then add the noodles, stock, 100ml (3½ fl oz) water, chilli sauce, soy and seasoning and heat through. Serve with the kebabs.

Spaghetti marinara

MAKES 4 PORTIONS

It's very important that you only buy very fresh seafood, so always buy it from a reputable source. This is a delicious pasta sauce and you can make it quite spicy for adults by adding more chilli if you like. I would not recommend giving seafood to very young children.

**PREP: 15 MINS,
PLUS SOAKING TIME
COOK: 15 MINS**

1 kg (2¼ lb) live mussels
350 g (12 oz) fresh clams
8 large raw prawns
250 g (9 oz) spaghettini

For the sauce
2 tbsp olive oil
4 shallots, finely chopped
1 garlic clove, crushed
2 tbsp chopped fresh parsley
6 tbsp dry white wine
2 × 400 g (14 oz) cans
    chopped tomatoes
1 or 2 dried chillies, finely
    chopped or a good pinch
    of crushed dried chillies
salt and black pepper

1 Discard any mussels or clams with cracked or open shells. Soak the mussels and clams in a large bowl of cold water for 20 minutes. Drain and give the mussels and clams a good wash and scrub them under cold running water using a stiff brush. Pull off any beards. Peel, devein and cut the prawns in half lengthways.

2 Cook the pasta in a large saucepan of lightly salted water according to the packet instructions.

3 Meanwhile, make the sauce: heat the olive oil in a frying pan and sauté the shallots and garlic for 2 minutes, add the parsley and sauté for 1 minute. Add the wine, simmer for 2 minutes, then add the tomatoes and chilli(es) and simmer for 4 minutes. Add the mussels and clams, cover and cook for 4–5 minutes. Discard any mussels or clams that do not open. Add the prawns and simmer for about 2 minutes and season to taste.

4 Drain the pasta, return to the warm pan, add the marinara sauce and toss gently. If you like, remove the mussels from their shells and mix with the pasta.

Mulligatawny chicken curry

MAKES 6 PORTIONS

A mild, deliciously flavoured chicken curry, this is a recipe that my mother used to make for me when I was a child. I like a pretty tame curry but you can always make it more fiery by using a medium or hot curry powder. Serve with plain rice and poppadums or try making your own naan breads (see opposite).

PREP: 15 MINS
COOK: 1¼ HOURS

1 chicken, cut into about 8 pieces
a little plain flour, for coating
vegetable oil, for frying
2 onions, chopped
2 tbsp mild curry powder
6 tbsp tomato purée
900 ml (1½ pints) chicken stock
1 cooking apple (about 225 g/
    8 oz), peeled, cored and
    thinly sliced
1 large carrot, thinly sliced
2 lemon slices
75 g (3 oz) sultanas
1 bay leaf
4 tsp light soft brown sugar
salt and black pepper

1 Preheat the oven to 180°C/350°F/Gas 4.

2 Trim any fat from the chicken and remove some of the skin. Coat the chicken with a little flour seasoned with salt and pepper. Fry in the oil until lightly golden, then drain on kitchen paper and place in a casserole dish.

3 Heat 2 tablespoons of oil in a frying pan and sauté the onions for about 10 minutes or until softened but not coloured.

4 Stir in the curry powder and the purée and cook for a further 2–3 minutes. Stir in 2 tablespoons of flour then stir in 300 ml (10 fl oz) of the stock.

5 Add the sliced apple, carrot, lemon slices, sultanas, bay leaf, brown sugar and the remaining stock. Season with salt and pepper. Pour the sauce over the chicken in the casserole, cover and cook in the oven for 1 hour. Remove the lemon slices and bay leaf, take the chicken off the bone and cut into pieces before serving.

Naan bread with sultanas

MAKES 5 SMALL NAAN BREADS

No Indian meal is complete without naan bread. This recipe tastes amazing when still warm from the oven, and is good for scooping up any leftover sauce from a curry.

PREP: 20 MIN,
PLUS RISING TIME
COOK: 7 MINS

250 g (9 oz) strong white flour
2 tsp caster sugar
½ tsp salt
7 g (¼ oz) packet dried yeast
150 ml (5 fl oz) warm milk
2 tbsp olive oil, plus extra
    for greasing
50 g (2 oz) sultanas,
    finely chopped
a little melted butter,
    plus extra to serve

1 Put the flour, sugar, salt and yeast into a mixing bowl. Add the milk and olive oil and mix together using a wooden spoon until a dough is formed. Tip the dough out onto a clean work surface and knead for about 8 minutes until you have a smooth dough.

2 Put the dough into an oiled bowl and cover with clingfilm. Leave in a warm place for about 1 hour until doubled in size.

3 Put the dough on a clean, lightly floured work surface and knead for a few minutes. Divide into 5 pieces. Roll out each ball to a thin circle. Put the chopped sultanas on one half of the dough. Brush the edge with a little water, then fold over the other half to make a parcel. Pinch the edges together. Re-roll the dough into an oval shape and brush with melted butter.

4 Preheat the grill to the highest setting. Put a flat baking sheet under the grill for 5 minutes to get very hot. Put the naan breads on the hot sheet, butter-side up, and grill for 2 minutes until golden and the naan bread has puffed up. Brush with a little extra butter to serve.

Onion and Gruyère tart

MAKES 8 PORTIONS

This is my favourite savoury tart; a delicious mix of slowly caramelised onions and Gruyère cheese. It's easy to make the Parmesan pastry with a food processor.

**PREP: 30 MINS,
PLUS CHILLING TIME
COOK: 50 MINS**
225 g (8 oz) plain flour,
    plus extra for dusting
125 g (8 oz) butter, cubed
30 g (1¼ oz) Parmesan cheese
1 medium egg, beaten

For the filling
a knob of butter
1 tbsp olive oil
500 g (1 lb 2 oz) onions,
    thinly sliced
4 large eggs
300 ml (10 fl oz) double cream
150 ml (5 fl oz) milk
200 g (7 oz) Gruyère cheese,
    grated
30 g (1¼ oz) Parmesan cheese,
    grated
salt and black pepper

1 Line a 24–25 cm (9½–10 in) deep round loose-bottom tart tin.

2 To make the pastry, put the flour, butter and Parmesan in a food processor. Whizz until it looks like breadcrumbs. Add the egg and 1 tablespoon of water and whizz until the mixture forms a ball. Roll out on a clean, lightly floured work surface and line the base and sides of the flan tin with the pastry. Set aside to chill in the fridge for 30–35 minutes.

3 Preheat the oven to 220°C/425°F/Gas 7. Prick the base of the flan pastry and line with baking paper and then baking beans. Blind bake the pastry for 10 minutes. Remove the beans and bake for a further 8–10 minutes until lightly golden, then place the pastry case on a baking sheet.

4 To make the filling, melt the butter and olive oil in a frying pan. Add the onions and fry over a medium–high heat for 5 minutes. Cover with a lid and gently simmer for 20 minutes until soft and golden brown. Spread onto the base of the tart.

5 Beat the eggs in a bowl. Add the cream and milk and season. Add the Gruyère, then pour into the case. Sprinkle with the Parmesan.

6 Reduce the oven to 180°C/350°F/Gas 4. Bake for about 30–35 minutes until lightly golden on top and set in the middle.

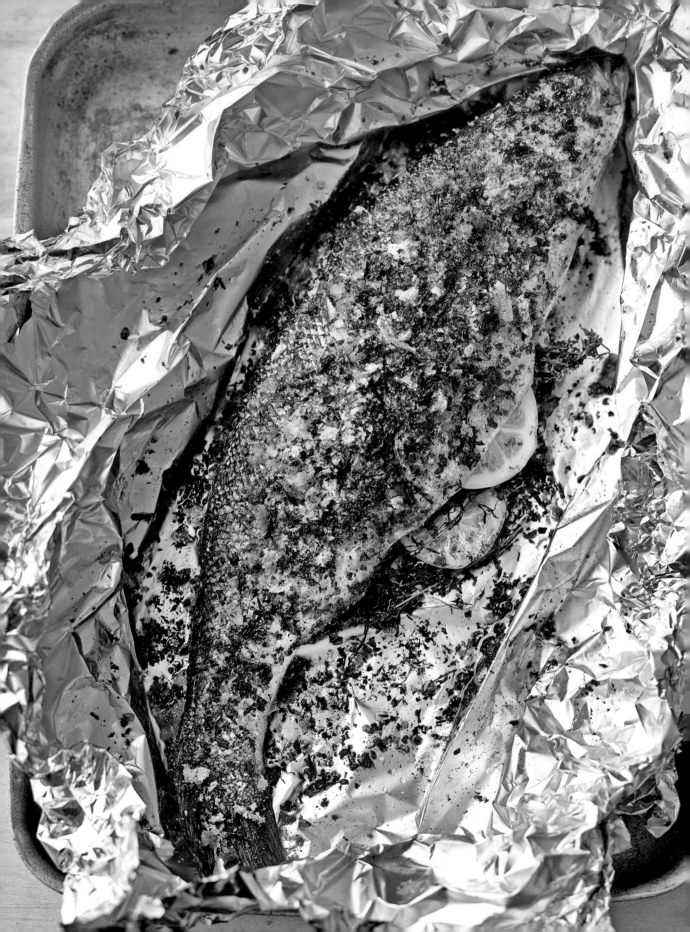

Baked seabass

MAKES 2 PORTIONS

One of the best ways to cook seabass is to wrap it in foil, which seals in the flavour and keeps the fish moist. I've flavoured the fish with lemon, parsley and thyme.

PREP: 10 MINUTES
COOK: 25–30 MINUTES

1 large seabass (enough for 2)
1 bunch of fresh thyme
1 lemon, halved and one
   half sliced
25 g (1 oz) butter, softened
15 g (½ oz) fresh breadcrumbs
2 tbsp chopped fresh parsley
a little paprika
salt and black pepper

1 Preheat the oven to 200°C/400°F/Gas 6.

2 Using a sharp knife, make 3 slashes along one side of the fish. Put half a bunch of thyme and 3 lemon slices into the belly of the fish. Chop 2 tsp of the remaining thyme and mix into the butter, then spread over and inside the slashes. Season to taste.

3 Wrap the seabass in a foil tent and squeeze over the juice of the remaining lemon half. Place the wrapped fish on a tray and roast in the oven for 15 minutes. Open the foil, sprinkle over the breadcrumbs, parsley and a little paprika, then put back into the oven for 10–15 minutes until lightly golden and cooked through.

Perfect paella

MAKES 4 PORTIONS

This paella is simple and quick to prepare. It is very important that
you use only fresh live mussels and any uncooked mussels that are already
open should be discarded. Once the mussels are cooked the shells should
open, but do not eat cooked mussels if the shells remain closed. You can
sometimes buy bags of frozen or fresh mixed seafood, which could also
be used for this recipe and then you may find that the mussels
are already cooked and out of their shells.

PREP: 10 MINS
COOK: ABOUT 35 MINS

1 tbsp olive oil
1 garlic clove, crushed
1 onion, chopped
1 red pepper, deseeded
  and cut into strips
300 g (11 oz) easy-cook rice
1 tsp turmeric
1 tsp mild chilli powder
1.2 litres (2 pints) chicken stock
1 bay leaf
2 tbsp chopped fresh parsley
250 g (9 oz) fresh prawns
225 g (8 oz) fresh clams
350 g (12 oz) live mussels
100 g (4 oz) frozen peas

1 Heat the olive oil in a saucepan and sauté the onion
and garlic for 1 minute. Add the red pepper and cook
for a further 3 minutes. Add the rice, turmeric and
chilli powder and stir for about 1 minute.

2 Pour in the stock, add the bay leaf and cook for
15 minutes over a medium heat. Add the parsley
and cook for about 5 minutes.

3 Turn the heat up, add the seafood and frozen peas
and cook for 1–2 minutes over a high heat. Reduce
the heat and cover and cook for about 5 minutes
or until the fish is cooked. Remove any shells that
haven't opened.

French beans with shallots

MAKES 4 PORTIONS (AS A SIDE DISH)

Fine French beans with sautéd shallots is an excellent flavour combination.

PREP: 5 MINS
COOK: ABOUT 8 MINS
400 g (14 oz) fine French beans
a knob of butter
2 shallots, sliced
1 garlic clove, crushed
1 tsp lemon juice
salt and black pepper

1 Slice the beans in half. Cook in a saucepan of salted boiling water for 4 minutes. Drain.

2 Melt the butter in a frying pan. Add the shallots and fry until soft. Add the garlic and beans and toss over the heat. Season and add the lemon juice.

Roasted vegetables

MAKES 4-6 PORTIONS

When you roast vegetables, something amazing happens: they become sweeter and a little caramelised. Serve these veg as a side dish to grilled meat or dish or toss them with pasta or wild rice to create a simple meal.

PREP: 10 MINS
COOK: 25-30 MINS

1 aubergine, cut into slices
2 courgettes, sliced
1 red pepper, deseeded and cubed
1 red onion, sliced
3 tbsp olive oil
1 garlic clove, crushed
1½ tsp fresh thyme leaves
2 tbsp balsamic vinegar
salt and black pepper

1 Preheat the oven to 180°C/350°F/Gas 4.

2 Put all the vegetables on a baking sheet. Toss with the olive oil, crushed garlic and thyme. Season to taste. Roast for 25–30 minutes until soft and tinged brown. Toss with the balsamic vinegar.

Bakes
and
sweets

Apple and carrot muffins

MAKES 12 MUFFINS

Here is a healthy and deliciously moist muffin that's bound to become a family favourite. These muffins are very easy to make and will keep well for up to five days.

PREP: 15 MINS
COOK: 20–25 MINS

150 g (5 oz) plain wholemeal flour
50 g (2 oz) granulated sugar
1½ tsp baking powder
½ tsp ground cinnamon
¼ tsp salt
¼ tsp ground ginger
125 ml (4 fl oz) vegetable oil
60 ml (2¼ fl oz) honey
60 ml (2¼ fl oz) maple syrup
2 medium eggs, lightly beaten
½ tsp vanilla extract
1 large apple, peeled, cored
   and grated
75 g (3 oz) carrots, peeled
   and grated
65 g (2½ oz) raisins

1 Preheat the oven to 180°C/350°F/Gas 4. Line a 12-hole muffin tray with paper cups.

2 Combine the flour, sugar, baking powder, cinnamon, salt and ginger in a mixing bowl.

3 In a separate bowl, combine the oil, honey, maple syrup, eggs and vanilla. Beat lightly with a wire whisk until blended. Add the grated apple, carrots and raisins to the liquid mixture and stir well.

4 Fold in the dry ingredients until just combined but don't overmix or the muffins will become heavy.

5 Fill the muffin cups with the batter until two-thirds full. Bake in the oven for 20–25 minutes. Leave the muffins to cool in the tin for 5 minutes before turning out onto a wire rack to cool completely.

Fruity oat bars

MAKES 18 BARS

These are good for lunchboxes or a tasty snack any time
and will keep for 1 week in an airtight container.

PREP: 10 MINS
COOK: 25 MINS

100 g (4 oz) unsalted butter
100 g (4 oz) light soft brown sugar
70 g (3 oz) golden syrup
150 g (5 oz) porridge oats
50 g (2 oz) dried cranberries,
  chopped
50 g (2 oz) raisins
50 g (2 oz) pecans, chopped
20 g (¾ oz) sunflower seeds

1 Preheat the oven to 180°C/350°F/Gas 4.

2 Put the butter, sugar and syrup in a saucepan and
heat until melted. Add the remaining ingredients and
mix until combined. Spoon into a 20 cm (8 in) square
non-stick baking tin and level the top.

3 Bake in the oven for 20 minutes until just firm
and lightly golden. Leave to cool for 5 minutes,
then slice into 18 bars.

Chocolate rice krispie squares

MAKES 16 SQUARES

These only take about 10 minutes to prepare and are very moreish –
a fun recipe to make with your children and ideal for lunch boxes.

PREP: 10 MINS,
PLUS CHILLING TIME
COOK: 5 MINS

75 g (3 oz) milk chocolate
50 g (2 oz) unsalted butter
3 tbsp double cream
100 g (4 oz) digestive biscuits,
    broken into small pieces
40 g (1½ oz) cranberries
50 g (2 oz) raisins
30 g (1 oz) Rice Krispies
40 g (1½ oz) chopped pecan nuts

1 Line a 20–23 cm (8–9 in) square tin with a strip
of non-stick baking paper.

2 Melt the chocolate, butter and cream in a heatproof
bowl over a pan of simmering water until runny. Don't
allow the base of the bowl to come into contact with
the water.

3 Add the biscuits, dried fruit, Rice Krispies and nuts.
Mix together then spoon into the tin and level the top.
Chill for 2 hours before cutting into small squares.
Store in the fridge for up to a week.

Chocolate and toffee marble cheesecake

MAKES 6 PORTIONS

This chilled, no-bake cheesecake has a beautifully soft texture. You can use toffee sauce or dulche de leche to create the marbled effect.

PREP: 30 MINUTES, PLUS CHILLING TIME

100 g (4 oz) digestive biscuits
50 g (2 oz) unsalted butter, melted
150 g (5 oz) full-fat cream cheese
200 ml (7 fl oz) whipped cream
150 g (5 oz) milk chocolate
2 tbsp toffee sauce
    (or dulce de leche)

1 Line an 18 cm (7 in) round loose-bottom cake tin with non-stick baking paper.

2 Crush the biscuits in a polythene bag with a rolling pin, then pour into a bowl and mix with the melted butter. Press the biscuits onto the base of the prepared tin and smooth with a spoon or potato masher. Leave to chill in the fridge.

3 Measure the cream cheese and cream into a bowl and whisk until thick.

4 Melt the chocolate in a heatproof bowl over a pan of simmering water until runny. Don't allow the base of the bowl to come into contact with the water. Leave to cool.

5 Divide the cream mixture in half. Add the chocolate to one half and the toffee sauce to the other, and mix well. Spoon the mixtures into the tin and gently swirl to make a marbled effect. Chill for 3 hours before serving.

Apricot cookies

MAKES 18 COOKIES

This fabulous and rather unusual combination of dried apricots
and white chocolate makes irresistible cookies. Once you have sampled
these you will probably want to double the quantities second time
around. These cookies will keep for 2 days but also freeze well.

PREP: 15 MINS
COOK: 15 MINS

100 g (4 oz) unsalted butter,
  softened
100 g (4 oz) cream cheese
100 g (4 oz) caster sugar
75 g (3 oz) plain flour
50 g (2 oz) chopped dried apricots
65 g (2½ oz) white chocolate
  chips or chopped white
  chocolate

1 Preheat the oven to 180°C/350°F/Gas 4. Line 2 baking
sheets with non-stick baking paper.

2 In a large mixing bowl, cream together the butter
and cream cheese. Add the sugar and beat until fluffy.
Gradually add the flour, then fold in the apricots and
chocolate. The dough will be quite soft – don't worry!
Drop the mixture by heaped teaspoons onto the
prepared baking sheets and bake in the oven for
15 minutes or until lightly golden. Leave to cool and
harden for a few minutes before removing them from
the baking sheet onto a wire rack to cool completely.

Strawberry cream cake

MAKES 8 PORTIONS

It looks impressive (see photo overleaf) but it is actually simple and quick to make; a classic Victoria sandwich-style cake filled with strawberries and whipped cream is wonderful for weekend teatime with family and friends.

**PREP: 30 MINS,
PLUS COOLING TIME
COOK: 20 MINS**
175 g (6 oz) soft margarine
175 g (6 oz) light soft brown sugar
3 large eggs, beaten
175 g (6 oz) self-raising flour
½ tsp lemon zest
1 tsp vanilla extract

For the filling/topping
300 ml (½ pint) whipping or
    double cream
3 tbsp icing sugar
150 g (6 oz) strawberries
2–3 tbsp strawberry jam

1 Preheat the oven to 180°C/350°F/Gas 4 and grease and line the bases of two 20 cm (8 in) sandwich tins.

2 Beat together the margarine and sugar, then add the eggs, one at a time, adding 1 tablespoon of flour with the eggs after the first egg to stop the mixture from curdling. Beat in the remaining flour, the lemon zest, vanilla and 1 tablespoon of water until light and fluffy.

3 Divide the mixture between the prepared sandwich tins and bake in the oven for about 20 minutes or until lightly golden and risen. Turn them out of the tins and put on a wire rack to cool.

4 To make the topping, whip the cream with the icing sugar until firm. Thinly slice 100 g (4 oz) of the strawberries. Stir the strawberries into two-thirds of the whipped cream. Spread the strawberry jam over one of the cakes, top with the strawberries and cream mixture and place the other cake on top. Using the remaining cream, pipe rosettes around the cake and place half a strawberry on top of each rosette. Keep refrigerated until ready to serve.

Chocolate and coffee cake

MAKES 8 PORTIONS

Coffee cake is one of my favourites treats and I love this combination of chocolate/ coffee sponge with coffee icing. You always get a much taller and more attractive cake if you split the sponges in half and layer them up with icing in between. Just make sure that the cakes are completely cool before carefully cutting them in half.

PREP: 25 MINUTES
COOK: 25–30 MINUTES, PLUS COOLING TIME

3 tbsp cocoa powder
2 tsp coffee granules
3 tbsp boiling water
4 medium eggs
225 g (8 oz) self-raising flour
225 g (8 oz) caster sugar
225 g (8 oz) unsalted butter, softened
2 tsp baking powder

For the coffee icing
250 g (9 oz) unsalted butter, softened
100 g (4 oz) cream cheese
350 g (12 oz) icing sugar
1 tbsp coffee granules
1 tbsp boiling water
plain chocolate for chocolate curls, to decorate

1 Preheat the oven to 180°C/350°F/Gas 4. Grease and base-line two 20 cm (8 in) round cake tins.

2 To make the cake, measure the cocoa, coffee and boiling water into a large bowl and stir until smooth, then add the remaining cake ingredients and, using an electric whisk, whisk until smooth.

3 Spoon the mixture into the prepared tins and level the top. Bake in the oven for 25–30 minutes until well risen and coming away from the sides of the tins. Leave to cool for a few minutes then remove from the tins and leave to cool completely on a wire rack. When cool, slice each cake in half with a serrated knife so that you have 4 even sponge layers.

4 To make the icing, whisk the butter and cream cheese together in a large bowl until fluffy. Add the icing sugar and whisk until fluffy. Mix the coffee with the water until it has dissolved, then add to the icing and stir well.

5 Put one of the cakes onto a serving plate. Spread over one-quarter of the icing, then continue to layer up, finishing with icing on the top. Decorate with chocolate curls to finish.

No-bake train cake

SERVES 20

The beauty of this cake is that it requires no cooking and can be created in very little time from basic ready-made ingredients. Older children will enjoy helping you assemble it but watch out that they don't eat the ingredients first as it's made out of all the things that children love. You can choose any selection of sweets for the goods carriages (see photo overleaf).

PREP: 50 MINS

For the grass
2 × 250 g (9 oz) packets of
  desiccated coconut
38 ml (1½ fl oz) edible
  green food colouring
5 tbsp apricot jam

For the chocolate buttercream
75 g (3 oz) unsalted butter,
  softened
125 g (4½ oz) icing sugar
1 tbsp cocoa powder
1 tbsp milk

5 × 205 g (7 oz) large chocolate-
  covered Swiss rolls filled
  with chocolate buttercream
1 milk chocolate marshmallow
  tea cake
1 chocolate Rolo
227 g (8 oz) packet Liquorice
  Allsorts
1 liquorice Catherine wheel
1 box chocolate sticks

1 To make the grass to cover the cake board, thoroughly mix the desiccated coconut with a little of the green food colouring and a few drops of water. Warm the apricot jam and brush it over the surface of two 40 × 30 cm (16 × 12 in) silver cake boards. The cake boards can be stuck together first if you like or if you are going to transport the cake, it's probably best if they are left separate. Strew the green coconut over the cake boards and press down on to the board so that they are completely covered.

2 To make the chocolate buttercream, beat the softened butter until creamy. Sift the icing sugar and cocoa powder into the bowl and beat together with the butter. Finally, beat in the milk.

3 Cut about 5 cm (2 in) off the end of one of the large chocolate Swiss rolls and secure this on top of a whole large chocolate Swiss roll to form the engine with some of the chocolate buttercream or a cocktail stick to form the cab. Secure a chocolate marshmallow tea cake with a Rolo to form the chimney. Attach 2 Liquorice Allsorts to form the windows of the cab. Attach a liquorice

2 × 150 g (5 oz) box milk
  chocolate fingers
20 milk chocolate-coated mini
  Swiss rolls
6 raspberry jam sandwich creams

150 g (5 oz) packet fizzy
  strawberry and cream flavour
  lances
100 g (4 oz) packet Dolly Mixtures
200 g (7 oz) packet mini
  marshmallows
2 packets mini assorted sweets

Catherine wheel to the front of the cab with some of the buttercream. If you like, attach cotton wool balls on to a length of wire to look like steam coming from the engine.

4 Lay out the track using two parallel lines of chocolate sticks in a zigzag pattern and lay milk chocolate fingers across the track to form the railway line. You will need to allow for the engine and five carriages. Put five mini milk chocolate rolls at the front of the track to form the bumper and the wheels of the engine and balance the engine on top. Attach three raspberry sandwich cream biscuits to each side of the engine with some of the buttercream to form the wheels and decorate the front with two Liquorice Allsorts. Cut a thin slice off the top of the remaining large chocolate Swiss rolls to form the carriages of the train and spread the flat surfaces with some of the chocolate buttercream. Lay each of the carriages over the mini Swiss rolls along the track. Pile the sweets onto the open trucks to finish.

Summer fruit brûlée with amaretto biscuits

MAKES 6 PORTIONS

This is one of my favourite desserts and is particularly good in summer when peaches and berry fruits are in season. You can also make this using other combinations of fruits – but it's important that the fruit should be really ripe and have a good flavour. Fruits that work well are mangoes, grapes, nectarines, strawberries, kiwi fruit. You could also mix in some passionfruit pulp if you like.

PREP: 10 MINS,
PLUS CHILLING TIME
COOK: 10 MINS

150 g (5 oz) blueberries
150 g (5 oz) raspberries
2 ripe juicy peaches, peeled, stoned and chopped
50 g (2 oz) amaretto biscuits, crushed
300 ml (½ pint) crème fraîche
1½ tbsp light muscovado sugar

1 Mix the fruit together and arrange in an ovenproof dish. Sprinkle the crushed amaretto biscuits on top and pour over the crème fraîche. Set aside in the fridge for at least 1 hour.

2 Preheat the grill to high. Sprinkle over the brown sugar and place under a the hot grill for a few minutes until golden.

Iced berries with hot white chocolate sauce

MAKES 4 PORTIONS

The slightly frozen berries melt into the warm chocolate
sauce giving a delicious contrast.

**PREP: 5 MINS,
PLUS FREEZING TIME
COOK: 5 MINS**

500 g (1 lb 2 oz) mixed frozen
  berries, eg blackberries,
  blueberries, raspberries,
  redcurrants

For the sauce
140 g (5 oz) white chocolate
142 ml (4½ fl oz) carton of
  double cream

1 Put the berries into a suitable container and place
in the freezer for 2 hours until semi-frozen.

2 Melt the white chocolate together with the double
cream in a heatproof bowl over a pan of simmering
water. Don't allow the base of the bowl to come into
contact with the water. Stir until the chocolate has
melted into the cream.

3 Scatter the frozen fruits on 4 plates or in shallow
bowls, pour over the hot chocolate sauce and serve
immediately.

Peach, raspberry and apple crumble

MAKES 5 PORTIONS

A really good crumble bursting with fruit is comfort food at its very best. Other good fruit fillings are rhubarb, gooseberry, blackberry and apple or strawberry and plum. Serve hot with vanilla ice cream or custard (see photo overleaf).

PREP: 20 MINS
COOK: 35–40 MINS

25 g (1 oz) unsalted butter
2 eating apples, peeled and sliced
3 tbsp light soft brown sugar
2 white peaches, stoned
   and chopped
250 g (9 oz) raspberries
3 tbsp ground almonds

For the topping
150 g (5 oz) plain flour
100 g (4 oz) cold unsalted
   butter, cut into pieces
75 g (3 oz) demerera sugar
25 g (1 oz) porridge oats

1 Preheat the oven to 200°C/400°F/Gas 6.

2 Melt the butter in a large pan and add the apples and sugar. Cook for 3–4 minutes then remove from the heat.

3 Add the chopped peaches and raspberries to the apples, then arrange in a shallow ovenproof dish (a round dish with a 17 cm/7 in diameter is ideal).

4 To make the topping, mix the flour with the butter, rubbing the mixture with your fingertips until it resembles breadcrumbs. Add the demerera sugar and porridge oats and mix. Cover the fruit with the crumble then bake in the oven for 30–35 minutes or until the topping is lightly golden.

Strawberry and lychee lollies

MAKES 6 LOLLIES

It's easy to make your own ice lollies using fresh or canned fruit. You can also make fresh fruit lollies simply by pouring fruit smoothies or pure fruit juice into an ice-lolly mould. This delicious ice lolly is so simple to make but was very popular with my children when they were small.

**PREP: 5 MINS,
PLUS FREEZING TIME**
425 g (15 oz) can lychees in syrup
150 g (5 oz) fresh strawberries, hulled and cut in half

1 Purée the lychees and syrup together with the fresh strawberries. Strain through a sieve. Pour into ice-lolly moulds and freeze for 4 hours or overnight until set.

Watermelon and strawberry lollies

MAKES 4 LOLLIES

You can also make a quick watermelon lolly by blending chopped, deseeded watermelon with a little icing sugar, before freezing the mixture in lolly moulds.

**PREP: 10 MINS,
PLUS FREEZING TIME**
300 g (11 oz) ripe watermelon, deseeded and diced
100 g (4 oz) strawberries, hulled and halved
3 tbsp Strawberry Ribena cordial

1 Put the melon and strawberries into a food processor and whizz until smooth. Pour into a jug. Add the cordial and pour into 4 lolly moulds. Place in the freezer for 4 hours or overnight until set.

Chocolate brownies with caramel sauce

MAKES 24

I like a mix of plain and milk chocolate in my brownies,
and I like them slightly undercooked too.

PREP: 20 MINUTES
COOK: 34–40 MINUTES
100 g (4 oz) milk chocolate
100 g (4 oz) plain chocolate
200 g (7 oz) unsalted butter
150 g (5 oz) caster sugar
4 medium eggs
50 g (2 oz) self-raising flour
30 g (1 oz) cocoa powder
icing sugar, for dusting

For the toffee sauce
50 g (2 oz) unsalted butter
50 g (2 oz) light soft brown sugar
200 ml (7 fl oz) double cream
½ tsp vanilla extract

1 Preheat the oven to 200°C/400°F/Gas 6. Line a 30 × 23 cm (12 × 9 in) tin with non-stick baking paper.

2 Melt the chocolates and butter in a heatproof bowl over a pan of simmering water until runny. Don't allow the base of the bowl to come into contact with the water. Add the remaining ingredients and whisk until smooth. Pour the mixture into the prepared tin and bake in the oven for 35–40 minutes until well risen and firm to the touch. Leave to cool in the tin, then cut into 24 squares and dust with icing sugar.

3 To make the toffee sauce, simply heat all the ingredients together in a saucepan until melted. Serve the brownies with the toffee sauce.

Cranberry and white chocolate cookies

MAKES 20 COOKIES

These are not to be missed: probably my favourite
cookies and so quick and easy to make.

PREP: 10 MINS
COOK: 12 MINS
150 g (5 oz) plain flour
½ tsp bicarbonate of soda
½ tsp salt
25 g (1 oz) ground almonds
150 g (5 oz) light soft brown sugar
50 g (2 oz) porridge oats
50 g (2 oz) dried cranberries
40 g (1½ oz) white chocolate,
 cut into chunks
150 g (5 oz) unsalted butter
1 large egg yolk or 2 small
 egg yolks

1 Preheat the oven to 190°C/375°F/Gas 5.

2 Sift together the flour, bicarbonate of soda and salt in a large bowl. Stir in the ground almonds, brown sugar, porridge oats, cranberries and white chocolate chunks.

3 Melt the butter in a small saucepan. Stir this into the dry ingredients together with the egg yolk. Mix well, then using your hands, form into walnut-sized balls and arrange on two large non-stick baking sheets. Gently press them down to flatten slightly, leaving space between them for the biscuits to spread.

4 Bake in the oven for 12 minutes, then remove and leave to cool on a wire rack.

Easy chocolate orange mousse

MAKES 6

The addition of creamy crème fraîche and tangy orange zest definitely gives this chocolate mousse the wow factor (see photo overleaf).

**PREP: 8 MINS,
PLUS CHILLING TIME
COOK: 5 MINS**
200 g (7 oz) plain chocolate
200 ml (7 fl oz) whipping cream
2 tbsp orange juice
1 tsp finely grated orange zest
100 g (4 oz) full-fat crème fraîche

1 Melt the chocolate in a heatproof bowl over a pan of simmering water until runny. Don't allow the base of the bowl to come into contact with the water. Leave to cook for 5 minutes.

2 Lightly whip the cream in a bowl. Add the orange juice and zest. Add the crème fraîche to the chocolate and stir until smooth. Fold into the whipped cream and spoon into 6 glasses. Chill for 1 hour before serving.

Tiramisu

This popular Italian dessert, known as a pick me up, is quick and
easy to prepare and is a great way to end a meal as it's very light. Serve
it in a glass bowl to show off the contrasting layers and textures.

**PREP: 20 MINS,
PLUS CHILLING TIME
COOK: 10 MINS**

2 tbsp strong instant coffee
  granules
1 tbsp brandy (optional)
16 Boudoir biscuits
300 ml (½ pint) good-quality
  ready-made custard
250 g (9 oz) mascarpone cheese
50 g (2 oz) caster sugar
1 tsp vanilla extract
150 g (5 oz) Amaretti biscuits
cocoa powder, for dusting

1 Measure the coffee into a jug and make up to 250 ml
(8 fl oz) with boiling water. Pour into a shallow dish.
Add the brandy (if using).

2 Soak the Boudoir biscuits in the coffee for 10 minutes,
then arrange in the base of a serving dish measuring
about 20 cm (8 in) in diameter.

3 Mix the custard, mascarpone, caster sugar and vanilla
together in a bowl. Pour over half of the mixture. Soak
the Amaretti biscuits in the coffee for 10 minutes and
arrange over the custard.

4 Pour over the remaining custard and level the top.
Sprinkle over the cocoa powder. Chill for 3 hours.

Vanilla cheesecake

MAKES 8 PORTIONS

It's hard to beat the taste of this New-York style, baked cheesecake, which I've topped with red fruits.

**PREP: 10 MINS,
PLUS CHILLING TIME
COOK: 40–45 MINS**

200 g (7 oz) digestive biscuits
100 g (4 oz) unsalted butter
1 tbsp caster sugar
600 g (1¼ lb) full-fat
  cream cheese
2 medium eggs
125 g (4½ oz) caster sugar
1 tsp vanilla extract
300 ml (½ pint) soured cream
3 tbsp seedless raspberry jam
250 g (9 oz) mix of raspberries
  and strawberries (halved)

1 Preheat the oven to 180°C/350°F/Gas 4. Base-line a loose-bottomed springform tin and grease the sides.

2 Crush the biscuits until they resemble fine crumbs (place in a larger freezer bag and crush with a rolling pin). Melt the butter in a large saucepan and stir in the crushed biscuits and sugar. Push into the base of the prepared tin and set aside in the fridge to chill while you make the filling.

3 Whisk the cream cheese in a bowl. Add the eggs, sugar, vanilla and soured cream and whisk until smooth. Pour into the tin and level the surface. Bake in the oven for 40–45 minutes until puffed up and set around the edges but with a slight wobble in the centre.

4 Leave to cool in the tin, then place on a serving plate. Warm the raspberry jam in a saucepan. Arrange the strawberries and raspberries on top of the cheesecake and drizzle with the slightly warm raspberry jam.

Caramelised pecan ice cream

SERVES 6

This ice cream tastes sensational, is very simple to make, contains no eggs and you don't need to use an ice cream machine. It goes well with fresh peaches, which can be served hot with some ice cream on the side. Simply wash and stone the peaches, cut in half, and sprinkle with a little brown sugar. Place under a preheated hot grill for a few minutes.

**PREP: 15 MINS,
PLUS FREEZING
AND COOLING TIME
COOK: 5 MINS**
410 g (14 oz) can evaporated milk
150 g (5 oz) caster sugar
300 ml (10 fl oz) double cream
2 tsp vanilla extract

For the caramelised pecans
225 g (8 oz) pecans
225 g (8 oz) light soft brown sugar

1 Pour the evaporated milk into a shallow dish and chill in the freezer for about 3 hours.

2 For the caramelised pecans, toast the nuts in a dry frying pan for a few minutes until golden, turning once. Put the brown sugar into a stainless steel saucepan together with 3 tablespoons of cold water and cook, stirring, over a gentle heat until it caramelises. Stir in the nuts and coat with the sticky caramel. Spread out on a baking tray to cool.

3 Once cool, place the caramelised pecans in a tea towel, wrap up and crush with a mallet or rolling pin. Whip the frozen milk with the caster sugar until thick. Whip the double cream and mix into the evaporated milk mixture together with the vanilla extract and the crushed pecans. Put into a suitable container and freeze for at least 4 hours until firm.

Red jelly

MAKES 6 PORTIONS

Making your own jelly is really easy using leaf gelatine. This is good on its own
or you can add some berry fruits. Serve in glasses or pour into a jelly mould.

**PREP: 20 MINS,
PLUS SETTING TIME**
5 leaves gelatine
200 ml (7 fl oz) strawberry cordial
400 ml (14 fl oz) red grape juice
300 g (11 oz) fresh mixed berries,
  e.g. blueberries, raspberries,
  strawberries (optional)

1 Soak the gelatine in a bowl of cold water for 5 minutes
until soft. Measure the cordial, grape juice and 200 ml
(7 fl oz) water into a saucepan. Squeeze out the water
from the gelatine using your hands and add to the
mixture. Heat and stir until dissolved.

2 Pour the jelly mixture into the glasses or mould.
Leave to cool then place in the fridge to set for about
6 hours or overnight.

3 If using fruit it's a good idea to set in two layers so
that the fruit remains at the bottom. Divide the fruit
between the glasses, pour over enough jelly to cover,
reserving the rest. Leave to cool then place in the fridge
to set lightly for about 3 hours. Top up with the
remaining jelly mixture.

Peach and summer berry fruit salad

MAKES 4 PORTIONS

Nothing beats a beautifully ripe peach but, if your fruit is slightly
hard or even a little overripe, it can come alive again in a fruit salad.
Vary the fruits to your own taste and the seasons.

PREP: 5 MINS
COOK: 3 MINS
a knob of unsalted butter
3 peaches, sliced
150 g (5 oz) blueberries
50 g (2 oz) caster sugar
225 g (8 oz) raspberries
150 g (5 oz) blackberries
100 g (4 oz) pomegranate seeds

1 Melt the butter in a saucepan. Add the peaches and
gently heat for 1 minute. Add the blueberries and sugar
and stir for 1 minute. Remove from the heat and add
the remaining fruits. Leave to cool before serving in
individual dishes.

Best-ever banana bread

MAKES 8 SLICES

This banana bread is wonderfully moist and is great for breakfast or lunchboxes. This keeps well (for up to 1 week) but you can also wrap slices in clingfilm and freeze in polythene freezer bags. You can easily omit the nuts from this recipe, if preferred.

PREP: 15 MINS
COOK: 1 HOUR
100 g (4 oz) unsalted butter, at room temperature
100 g (4 oz) brown sugar
1 medium egg
450 g (1 lb) bananas, mashed
3 tbsp natural yoghurt
1 tsp vanilla extract
225 g (8 oz) plain flour
1 tsp bicarbonate of soda
1 tsp ground cinnamon
¼ tsp salt
100 g (4 oz) raisins
40 g (1½ oz) chopped pecans or walnuts (optional)

1 Preheat the oven to 180°C/350°F/Gas 4. Grease a 22 × 11 × 7 cm (8½ × 4¼ × 2¾ in) loaf tin and line the base with non-stick baking paper.

2 Beat the butter and sugar together until creamy then add the egg and continue to beat until smooth. Add the mashed bananas, yoghurt and vanilla essence.

3 Sift together the flour, bicarbonate of soda, cinnamon and salt and beat this gradually into the banana mixture. Finally, stir in the raisins and chopped nuts (if using).

4 Bake in the oven for about 1 hour or until a cocktail stick inserted in the centre comes out clean. Leave to cool in the tin for 5 minutes before turning out onto a wire rack to cool completely.

Index

annabel karmel

Visit my website for further recipes, tips and advice on feeding your family, plus lots of great offers, competitions and more.

annabelkarmel.com

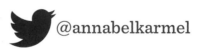 @annabelkarmel   f Annabelkarmeluk

. . . .

And now you can tap into Annabel's recipes and expertise whilst on the go.

Download Annabel's Essential Guide to Feeding Your Baby and Toddler to your iPhone, iPad or iPod Touch for lots of family food inspiration.

It offers instant access to 200 delicious recipes for little ones and the whole family, as well as features such as weekly planners, shopping lists, a kitchen timer, recipe notes and videos.

Want the latest news from Annabel and all your other favourite chefs?

Are you always on the look-out for new recipe inspiration?

Then join us at

Annabel Karmel MBE is just one of a stellar line-up of cooks and chefs that make up The Happy Foodie. A cookery community for food lovers, featuring recipes, interviews, tasty tips and culinary secrets from top chefs including Jamie Oliver, Nigella Lawson, Delia Smith, Mary Berry, Yotam Ottolenghi, Rachel Khoo and Rick Stein. Go behind the scenes and into the experts' kitchens with exclusive interviews, even more recipes, competitions and tips, mouthwatering special offers on a wide range of cookery books and, of course, much more from Annabel herself.

Visit thehappyfoodie.co.uk

@TheHappyFoodie   thehappyfoodie

Acknowledgements

Huge thanks to Fiona MacIntyre and Lizzy Gray for believing in my success in the world of adult cookery after 22 years of writing cookery books on how to mash a carrot.

Lucinda McCord for recipe testing and being such a wonderful support even when baby no. 2 was about to make an entrance. Sarah Smith, my amazing PR, who gets my life organised and makes me giggle at some of the crazy things we do together.

Martin Poole for his stunning photography and for coming off his no carb diet to 'test' my recipes. Emma, Alex and the team at Smith & Gilmour for designing the book so beautifully and being so hospitable when Hamilton, Bono and Sabre ran havoc at the photo shoot. Annie Rigg and Laura Fyfe for their wonderful food styling and Lydia Brun for bringing the food to life with her wonderful props and styling. Laura Higginson, my editor, for realising that when I said to put the evaporated milk in the freezer that I meant pour it from the can first. Naraa Allardyce and Angel Ivan for their help in making me look presentable on the photo-shoot day.

Stephen Margolis who was happy that for once this was not a book on baby purees and so, for a change, he had to chew his dinner. Nicholas, Lara and Scarlett for laughing at me and asking for take away. My mum for saying everything tasted delicious even when it didn't.

Everyone at Ebury for the chance to prove myself in the world of grown ups.

bolognese sauce Yakitori chicken with noodles
drumsticks Iced berries with hot white choc
Steak with tarragon and mushroom sauce
asy chocolate orange mousse Salad and soy dres
heesecake Chicken schnitzel Potato and chicken rosti
Squash, pea and sage risotto Tiramisu Salmon
mousse Caramelised onion and gruyere tart
at bars Tarragon chicken casserole
voury muffins Annabel's 15-minute tomato sauce
Chicken with summer vege
Welsh rarebit Easy beef casserole Chocolate rice krisp
Mulligatawny chicken curry Mini muffin pizz
Homemade naan
Summer risotto Chicken karmel Teriyaki chic
Marinated grilled chicken Jewelled couscous salad Ta
a melt Sweetcorn and broccoli fritters M
Perfect paella Finger licking drumsticks
basil Annabel's apricot cookies Cheese, c
rs Tasty 10-minute prawn stir Roast chicken
Strawberry and peach smoothie
fish Annabel's granola Roast leg of lamb
Lasagne with spinach, cheese and tomat
Gratin of courgette Honeyed lamb cutlets Tagliatelle with prawn
sandwich Chicken pasta salad Whole seal
a tagliatelle Sesame beef stir fry Yummy burger
Mini fish pies
Watermelon and strawber
vourite chicken and potato salad Chicken, tomat
Beef bourguignon with dumplings Onion soup
nara Thai-style chicken soup Med veg
nd cheese panini Meatballs in tomato and basil sauce
um tomatoes and basil Apple and carrot muffin
prawn pasta bows Vegetarian sausages Fruit salad
Posh fish fingers Perfect pancakes Mozzarell
Mediterranean tomato soup Multi-layered cottage pi
Vegetable fusilli Chicken fajitas Green
ty chicken burgers Chick